FORD GT40

John Allen

CONTENTS

Foulis

Haynes

Titles in the *Super Profile* series

Austin-Healey 'Frogeye' Sprite (F343)

Ferrari 250GTO (F308)

Ford GT40 (F332)

Jaguar D-Type & XKSS (F371)

Jaguar Mk 2 Saloons (F307)

Lotus Elan (F330)

MGB (F305)

Morris Minor & 1000 (ohv) (F331)

Porsche 911 Carrera (F311)

Further titles in this series will be published at regular intervals. For information on new titles please contact your bookseller or write to the publisher

ISBN 0 85429 332 9

A FOULIS Motoring Book

First published 1983

Published by:
Haynes Publishing Group
Sparkford, Yeovil,
Somerset BA22 7JJ

Distributed in USA by:
Haynes Publications Inc.
861 Lawrence Drive, Newbury Park, California 91320, USA

Editor: Rod Grainger
Dust jacket design: Rowland Smith
Page Layout: Madaleine Bolton
Printed in England by: J.H.Haynes & Co. Ltd

FOREWORD

When the Ford GT was unveiled to the public in April 1964, no one could have foreseen the extent of the problems that would have to be overcome to make it successful, nor the extent of that success when finally it arrived. For a racing car to be competitive for just one season is achievement enough, but for a car to remain competitive into its *sixth* season, rounding off its career with a spectacular victory at Le Mans, was previously unheard of.

The GT40, as it came to be known, was originally intended to be built in small numbers to supply Ford's racing effort; by the time production ceased in 1969, over 100 examples had been built, and many of these had found their way from the track to the road, providing their owners with the ultimate street car. Not since the Jaguar D-type-derived XKSS had there been a Le Mans winner adapted for everyday use, but the GT40 proved that the transformation was appropriate when production was resumed in 1981, the new Mark V being more than a match for the very best on offer from Ferrari, Porsche and others in terms of performance and road manners. And if the car is rather hard riding, could perhaps use a little more ground clearance, has less than average visibility and is, well, quite noisy, who could not forgive it?

During preparation of this *Super Profile,* I talked with a great many people who had in some way been involved with the GT40 story, from the design stage to the present day, and I am grateful to them for their help and co-operation. My especial thanks go to Ronnie Spain, whose detailed GT40 Register enabled me to contact many owners of whom I would otherwise have been unaware. The Ford Motor Company's photographic files have been invaluable, Steve T Clark and Edward J Sawtell locating for me pictures which for years I had sought elsewhere. Henri Bercher helped, putting his extensive collection of photographs at my disposal.

Thanks are also due to Len Bailey, John Horsman, John Etheridge, Bill Pink, Peter Thorp, Jim Rose, Bryan Wingfield, Richard J Kopec, Robert J Horne, John Harrison, Peter Sutcliffe, Dean Jeffries, and Brian Angliss. The GT40 owners who kindly sent me photographs of their cars are named in the appropriate captions. I am grateful to Steven Smith, who valiantly agreed to submit to an interrogation for the Owner's View Section!

Finally, I would like to thank *Autocar* for permission to reproduce Innes Ireland's track test of a GT40, and Ziff-Davis Publishing Co for permission to use the *Car & Driver* road test of a Mark III.

John S. Allen

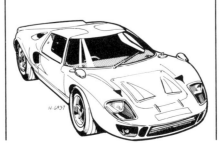

HISTORY

The dawning of the nineteen-sixties found the giant Ford Motor Company in search of a new image. The cars they were building were solid and reliable, but they lacked that ingredient which Lee Iacocca, Ford Division General Manager, referred to as *"pizzazz"*. Like many companies before them, Ford determined that the best way to inject flair and excitement into their name was to embark on a racing programme. To make such a decision was not easy, because Ford, as a member of the Automobile Manufacturers Association, was bound by the AMA's June 1957 agreement to eschew motor sport. Ford therefore renounced that agreement, and proceeded to embrace motor racing with fervour ....

One of the company's principal material assets in its entry into the fray was a lightweight, thinwall V8 of 260 cubic inches displacement (4261cc), which proved itself remarkably adaptable to various forms of competition. Recast in aluminium, and with overhead camshafts replacing its regular pushrods, the engine was ideal for powering an Indianapolis car, and proved it by taking the first four places at Indianapolis in 1965. The aluminium versions were reduced in size to 255 CID to comply with USAC regulations for Indianapolis cars, but the original 260 CID cast iron version was not overlooked — things were moving, down in California.

One time chicken farmer, and former racing driver, Carroll Shelby had been forced to end his racing career in 1960, when heart trouble was diagnosed. Shelby, born in Dallas, Texas, had begun racing in 1953, and had driven one of John Wyer's Aston Martin DBR-1s to that marque's only Le Mans victory, in 1959. After a short spell totally outside motorsport, Shelby moved to California and opened a racing drivers' school. Back in contact with the sport, he set about realising his dream of building a top flight sports car, and since Ford's small block V8 was one of the best engines going, Shelby acquired an early 221 CID model to provide the motive power for the car that was to become the Cobra.

With the co-operation of both AC Cars and of Ford, the AC Ace was modified by Shelby to take the 260 V8 which, in its high-performance road version, was rated at 260bhp. Only 75 of the Cobras were to receive that engine, for the 260 was enlarged into the legendary 289 — as light as its predecessor but even tougher. The Cobra proved to be an outstandingly successful car, the blend of British chassis design and American horsepower producing a combination that was difficult to beat, and Shelby's dream can be said to have been realised when, in 1965, the streamlined Cobra Daytona Coupes won the GT class in the World Manufacturers Championship.

As the Cobras set out upon the victory trail, Ford were enjoying the publicity, and the much needed *"pizzazz"* was spilling over to Ford's production cars. Unfortunately, too many people could claim an interest in the Cobra; Ford called it a Ford, Shelby called it a Shelby, and AC were not to be left out either. Ford also wanted an interest in a car with more *class* than had the Cobra. The Cobra was bold and brash, and about as safe and friendly as its reptilian namesake; in short, it was a brute.

The higher echelons at Ford wanted a car with the finesse and elegance of a Ferrari, and, in a most extraordinary series of negotiations, very nearly bought the entire Ferrari Company. The death of Ferrari's son, Dino, had left Enzo without an heir, and, at the age of 65, Ferrari was concerned about the future of his company. The deal which was worked out between Ferrari and Ford would have given Ford control over the production of Ferrari road cars, to be called "Ford-Ferrari", leaving racing in the hands of Ferrari himself, the racing cars to be called, predictably, "Ferrari-Fords". That the deal did not go through was possibly a Good Thing for Ford, for any creditable achievement of the cars would more than likely have been ascribed to Ferrari, whilst failures would have resulted in Ford receiving the blame.

Lee Iacocca then took the momentous decision that Ford would build its own racing car with which to compete with Ferrari. It was more easily said than done, because Ford had no experience of building racing cars, and there was a dearth of competent chassis designers in the USA. Attention then turned to England, where the required expertise existed. Three companies came under scrutiny: Cooper, Lola and Lotus, and of these Lola seemed most promising. Lola Cars Ltd. was owned and controlled by Eric Broadley, and already had produced a modern sports-racing car which would be an ideal springboard for the Ford GT project. The Lola GT was mid-engined, had a composite semi-monocoque chassis, and used Ford's ubiquitous 260 power plant. A deal with Eric Broadley was swiftly concluded and, until a new company (Ford Advanced Vehicles) was formed and premises obtained, the Ford contingent moved into the Lola works at Bromley.

Heading Ford's design team was Englishman Roy Lunn, who had been with Ford in America for several years; Broadley was to be responsible for overall design and production, whilst administration was in the hands of John Wyer, who had been recommended for the post by Shelby. Chassis design was entrusted to Len Bailey, another Englishman, and one who is still closely involved with the GT40. Design and construction of the prototype GT40 then went ahead at the Lola factory, before moving to the new premises in Slough towards the end of 1963. Testing was helped by Ford having acquired two of the three Lola GTs built, and using them as experimental mules for trying out new components.

The first Ford GT was completed on April 1st, 1964, and was promptly airlifted to the USA in time for the New York Show that month. The development time so wasted was to be sorely missed ....

Design

The prototype Ford GT embodied some unusual design features, which set the car apart from its contemporaries. The chassis was a semi-monocoque in sheet steel, at a time when many racing cars were built out of aluminium tubing. The steel structure was immensely strong, as it proved later when bigger and considerably heavier engines were fitted, but the use of steel imposed a weight penalty which was to handicap the car throughout its career. The structure included substantial roll-over protection built into the rear bulkhead, which was extended forward from the top centre to meet the windscreen and form the roof. The closed coupe arrangement also helped strengthen the chassis more than would have been possible with a roadster. The doors were cut well into the roof to assist rapid entry to the cockpit, so saving valuable seconds in a Le Mans start.

The fuel was housed in two tanks incorporated in the chassis' very wide sills. Bag tanks were used, to avoid the sealing problems which can occur in welded units, capacity being 140 litres (30.5 Imperial gallons), the maximum permitted by Appendix J to the International Sporting Code. Considerable use was made of computers in establishing the suspension geometry, enabling the new car to be immediately competitive, despite its short pedigree. A novel feature was the front air-dam or spoiler, placed beneath the fairly high but smoothly streamlined nose. The spoiler was developed during wind tunnel testing at the University of Maryland, using a $\frac{3}{8}$ scale model, and was found both to reduce drag and, more significantly, aerodynamic lift. The spoiler was small by today's standards, and incorporated a pair of long range lights which supplemented the main rectangular lights faired into the nose section.

The bodywork was in fibreglass, both nose and tail sections being fully removable to aid access. The nose featured two small triangular vents in the upper surface, these being intended to assist the flow of cooling air and to prevent the build up of pressure which could cause lift. It was anticipated that speeds of 200mph would be reached, and considerable effort was spent on designing the bodywork so as to keep lift at a minimum, with little success at first. The rear bodywork was of gently sloping fastback design, incorporating a perspex window which, although in keeping with the letter of the regulations, was so nearly horizontal as to offer only minimal rearward vision. Following the theories developed by Professor W Kamm in the 1930s, the tail was chopped off at the point where airflow separation began, the bodywork curving down to be hinged at the bottom.

A most complicated series of ducts was employed to take air in at the high pressure areas at the front and supply it to where it was needed, at the back. Intakes at the base of the screen fed through the bulkhead to the doors, which themselves contained ducting leading to holes in the rear bulkhead, through which the air entered the engine compartment. External ducts, immediately in front of the rear wheels, fed cooling air to the brakes. The interior was ventilated by means of the ducts at the base of the screen, air being piped to the seats, which contained their own ducting and outlet vents, and to adjustable dashboard vents. It was thought most important to ensure that driver comfort was maximised, thus reducing fatigue during long races.

The original car was powered by the aluminium V8 developed for Indianapolis, and displacing 255 cubic inches; the pushrod version was used initially, but it was intended that ultimately, the four-cam engine would be fitted. The engine's dry sump configuration necessitated the use of a separate oil tank, which was fitted in the nose, and which was of an unusual shape, forming the cradle in which the spare wheel was carried. A pipe from the uppermost part of the tank carried the filler cap, which was accessed through a hole in the top of the front bodywork. The oil cooler was integral with the radiator, which was front mounted, coolant pipes taking water through the centre of the cockpit to the engine at the back. The mid-engined layout was by no means new, but was still to be universally adopted, with Aston Martin and Maserati still producing front-engined prototypes. One of the most difficult problems faced by the design team was the provision of a suitable transmission, capable of handling the torque produced by the 4.2-litre engine. A Colotti 4-speed, non-synchromesh, gearbox was chosen, although there was doubt as to its ability to accept the V8's torque with reliability; however, no other available transmission was stronger, so the

Colotti had to do until the gearbox being developed by the German firm of ZF was in production.

The driveshafts featured inboard Metalastic joints, dubbed "rubber doughnuts" which helped to cushion the transmission, but were also looked upon as a potential weak point. Brakes were solid discs, those at the rear being mounted outboard due to lack of space alongside the transaxle. Borrani wire wheels were chosen, as they were expected to allow for better brake cooling than would disc wheels, although they were heavy and of questionable durability. Of 15-inch diameter, they carried Dunlop tyres on rim widths of $6\frac{1}{2}$ inches (front) and 8 inches (rear).

Development

Initial testing of the cars showed that they overheated badly, and their beautifully smooth nose sections had to be quickly and roughly opened up with three vents, these subsequently being joined up to form one long intake. The first two cars were whisked off to Le Mans for the 1964 Test Weekend, where they proved almost undriveable at speed. The aerodynamics which had worked so well on small-scale models in the wind tunnel were woefully inadequate in a full size car on the track: the body shape developing so much lift that the first car was written off when it tried to become airborne at the kink of the Mulsanne straight. The second car was slightly damaged in a minor accident, and the team, somewhat shaken, then returned to Slough. Fortunately the problem of lift was cured easily and quickly, by adding a small spoiler across the rear, and fairing it into the bodywork. The cooling problems were not so easily solved, and the nose design was repeatedly modified in an attempt to combine low drag with adequate airflow to the radiator. It was not until the middle of 1965 that the

definitive nose section appeared, being used with only minor differences on all subsequent models. The complicated ducting was scrapped when it was discovered, in later wind tunnel testing, that 76bhp was being absorbed by it.

The 1964 season was not a happy one for Ford, with the cars failing to finish in every race they entered; one of the main sources of trouble was the notorious Colotti gearbox, which proved that it simply was not strong enough, and was replaced by the new ZF as soon as the latter became available. Shortage of aluminium engines led to the adoption, on a trial basis, of the cast iron 289 inch (4.7-litre) unit, with wet-sump lubrication. The engine was more powerful than its predecessor, and gave more torque. As its weight was only slightly higher than the 255, it became used as standard; it did, however, suffer from head gasket problems which were not solved until the advent of the Gurney-Weslake cylinder heads in 1968.

Whilst Ford Advanced Vehicles in England persevered with the 289, concentrating on its development, and letting Shelby spearhead the 1965 racing effort, an altogether more awesome beast was being born. Two chassis from the 1965 prototype batch were shipped to Dearborn, where, in the Ford-owned Kar Kraft facility they received the mighty 427 cubic inch 7-litre engine. The resulting car was even heavier than the already weighty standard car, but with some 465bhp on tap it was remarkably fast, lapping the Ford test track in Michigan at a resounding 200mph!

Whilst the 7-litre cars, later dubbed Mk II, were being built, Ford Advanced Vehicles embarked on the construction of a series of at least fifty production cars for sale to private customers for use on both road and track. The GT40, so called because of its 40 inch height, was intended to secure the sports car championship, while the Mark II

was to be the ultimate weapon for securing the badly needed Le Mans victory.

The start of 1966 saw the GT40 still in production, but with official emphasis being placed on the Mark II to spearhead the Le Mans attack. The problems facing the Mark II were even more severe than those previously encountered by the GT40, for the big engine and the increased speed potential put considerable extra strain on many areas of the car. The brakes were a main cause for concern, as slowing the bulky Mk II from 210mph to 30mph at Mulsanne corner every three and a half minutes was quite beyond the capability of the GT40 brakes. The units eventually installed were $\frac{3}{4}$ inch thick ventilated discs of $11\frac{1}{2}$ inches diameter, which were made easily removable to facilitate changes if cracking occurred during a race. The rear brakes were cooled by means of air drawn in through large scoops mounted high on the rear bodywork, immediately aft of the bulkhead, and which became the Mark II's most obvious identification feature. For some races these scoops were supplemented by periscope-like protruberances in the centre of the rear deck. Finding a gearbox which would accept the torque of the Mark II's 7-litre engine proved impossible, so Ford set out to built their own, using internals from the four speed unit in production for the Galaxie. Very little trouble was encountered with the unit, although at Daytona in 1967 every Mark II present suffered transmission failure due to faulty heat treatment of output shafts.

The Mark II's weight resulted in some unexpected problems. During practice for the 1966 Daytona Continental, the cars were compressing their suspensions so much on the banking that the offside front wheels began to wear through the bodywork. A temporary solution was achieved by cutting away the offending bodywork but, as the regulations demanded that the wheels be covered, fibreglass domed patches were placed over the holes for the race itself. All subsequent Mk IIs featured modified nose sections with raised areas above the wheels, resulting in a distinctive hunched appearance.

Leaving the British to experiment with alloy bodywork and open-topped cars, America's answer to the weight problem was to design a totally new car, using a bonded aluminium monocoque, and an automatic transmission which had been tried briefly in Mark IIs; the GTP, nicknamed "J-car" was developed into the Mark IV, which would become Ford's principal weapon for 1967.

Victory at Le Mans

The Mark II succeeded in giving Ford its desperately needed Le Mans victory in 1966, and no one would have blamed Ford if they had pulled out of racing there and then. To their credit, they elected to try to prove that their first victory was no mere flash in the pan. During the winter of 1966/67 most of the development effort went into the J-car/Mark IV, but the trusty Mark II was refined to provide back-up in case the J-car project could not be made to work. The new car, known as the Mk IIB, featured several improvements over the previous year's model, retrospectively referred to as the Mark IIA. Cast iron cylinder heads for the 427 replaced aluminium ones, and the engine received a second carburettor, power being about 500bhp, or 15bhp more than the previous year. The front brake ducts were closed off, with air for the brakes being taken from behind the radiator. Although this naturally reduced the cooling effect, the discs were less prone to cracking than if they were fed with cold air from outside. The periscope ducts for the rear brakes were removed too. Inside the car, the passenger seat was used as a location for the newly developed fire-extinguishing

system, using both gravity and infra-red sensors; despite the regulations insisting that the passenger seat should be kept clear, race organisers were sensible enough to turn a blind eye to this breach of the rules. A further change involved the placement of the spare wheel, which was mounted alongside the transmission at the rear of the vehicle.

The Mark IIB was not the only newcomer in 1967. Ford Advanced Vehicles' assets had been sold off to J W Automotive Engineering Limited, headed by John Wyer and sponsored by Gulf Oil. JW produced the ultimate lightweight GT40 in the shape of the Mirage M1, which used basic GT40 chassis and mechanical parts, but featured a much narrower upper cockpit section and smoother bodywork.

The GT40 story very nearly came to an abrupt and premature end as 1967 closed, for the sport's ruling body, the FIA, announced capacity limits of 3-litres for prototypes and 5-litres for Group 4 Sports Cars, which had to have been produced in quantities of at least 50 units. The prototype limit effectively made the Mark II obsolete overnight, but there were those who believed that the GT40 stood a reasonable chance of being competitive when pitted against the 3-litre prototypes. Ford had already announced their intention of withdrawing from sports car racing, so it was left to J W Automotive to turn the GT40 into a race winner. This task was nothing new for John Wyer who, with Gulf sponsorship, commenced the production of a small series of GT40s incorporating the lessons learned from the Mirage project.

The Gulf GT40s started life with the regular 289 engines, these being soon stretched to 4942cc (302 CID) to make maximum use of the capacity allowed by the regulations. The most significant advance incorporated by these cars was the adoption of Gurney-

Weslake cylinder heads, finally curing the head gasket problems which had plagued the small-block Ford since its introduction to racing. Experiments with dry-deck cylinder heads, where the water passages between head and block were sealed up, were conducted, with poor results. The replacing of internal water passages by external pipes did prevent the failure of gaskets, but resulted in steam pockets being formed, these leading to failures in the blocks themselves. Gurney-Weslake-powered Gulf Ford GT40s represented the ultimate variation on the GT40 theme, and with some 465bhp available in the 1969 model, were surprisingly fast. It is interesting to compare their performance at Le Mans with that of the Mark II, which made its fastest lap there in 1967, with Paul Hawkins turning in a time of 3 minutes 25.8 seconds. The best showing by a Gulf GT40 was in 1968, after the track had been modified by the inclusion of the Ford Chicane immediately before the pits, and which was reckoned to cost some 10 to 12 seconds per lap. Ickx, during testing for the 1968 event, turned an easy 3 minutes 35.4 seconds, showing that a well-sorted GT40 would have been a match for a Mark II.

Road Cars

It is inevitable that with a car like the GT40, racing versions will steal the limelight. The road car project had begun with the 1965 production series, as it was felt that the car offered considerable potential in the making of an exclusive high-performance sports car for the wealthy connoisseur. Differences between road and race specifications were minor, and it was not unknown for "Road" cars to take part in international race events. Most road cars used a detuned version of the 289 engine, the four Weber carburettors sometimes being replaced by a single four-barrel Holley, in the interests of both tractability and ease of maintenance, power being quoted as 335bhp. The clutch was less harsh, and a heavier flywheel helped smooth progress. Inside the car some concessions were made towards road use, but the trim used was generally not of a high standard, prompting attention from specialist coachbuilders Graber in Switzerland and Wood & Pickett in the UK, both firms retrimming the car to much higher standards.

Many road equipped GT40s were sold in the USA, but problems were met both in the right hand drive layout and in complying with America's legal requirements. In an attempt to enable the GT40 to be enjoyed by a wider clientele, the Mark III model was introduced late in 1966. The most significant alteration in the Mark III was the provision of a central gearchange, in place of the previous right hand change, thus enabling left hand drive to be incorporated. Unfortunately, the shift linkage had to follow a tortuous path to find its way past the engine and into the ZF gearbox, and lost much of its precision as a result.

The Mark III featured several other improvements over the basic road cars. The Derrington-designed "bundle of snakes" exhaust was replaced by a much simplified system, wherein the pipes were kept low, with no crossover used, to exit at the base of the rear bodyshell. This system cost some power, but allowed a luggage box to be fitted in the elongated tail, above the gearbox. While the box was not large, and tended to absorb heat from the nearby engine and gearbox, it was still a welcome feature. At the front of the car the bodywork was raised slightly, and reprofiled to accept four circular lamps in place of the two rectangular units previously employed, enabling compliance with various US State laws. The suspension was altered, the springs being about 30% softer than on the Mark I, and comfort was further

improved by re-routing the coolant pipes outside the cockpit, rather than down the centre.

Road cars were sold in the UK at prices from £7,254 to £7,539. These figures seem small by current standards and, lest the enthusiast should now be gnashing his teeth at the thought of a bargain missed, it is worth bearing in mind what those sums would have bought in 1969. Ford put the price in perspective in their double page advertisements that year: beneath a colour photograph of a road car was the caption "Would you let your daughter marry a Ford owner? The Ford GT40 £7,539. 0-60mph: 6 secs. 1st gear: 58mph. Top gear: 164mph. Boot space: laughable. Petrol consumption: wicked. If you're a bit worried about your future son-in-law just ponder over the trade-in value: 5 Escorts, plus 3 Cortina Estates, plus a Corsair 2000. You could become the first 9 car family in your road".

By 1969 the GT40 was, with minor exceptions, outclassed in international sports car racing, and sale of road cars had slowed to a trickle, the Mark III never really being accepted by those lucky enough to be able to afford it. Production by J W Automotive ceased that year after the 7th Mark III and the 85th production car from the Mark I/II series.

The GT40 in Motorsport

Nobody expected the GT40 to be a winner right from the start, but its first season of competition was unbelievably bad. From ten starts the cars scored ten retirements, mostly due to gearbox failures; there was no lack of speed or handling, the cars always being impressively fast, but reliability was virtually non-existent. Apart from the gearbox maladies, GT40s gave notice of troubles to come when the Attwood/Schlesser car (104) caught fire at Le Mans when a fuel line broke; at least nine other

GT40s have subsequently been damaged or destroyed by fire.

The 1964 debacles prompted Ford to re-assess the entire GT40 programme, and the decision was taken to transfer the car's racing activities from Ford Advanced Vehicles to Shelby American. At first it looked as if the problems had been solved, for the 1965 season opened with GT/103 winning the Daytona 2000km race, GT/104 placing third in the same event. The 12-hour race duration had proved to be within the cars' capabilities thanks to their Colotti gearboxes having been substantially strengthened since the end of 1964. The Shelby team followed up this victory by a second place in the 1965 Sebring 12-hour race, before the two cars were shipped to Europe for the remainder of the season. In Europe, the cars once again failed miserably, being no faster than the Ferraris ... and far less reliable.

For Le Mans in 1965, Ford's hopes were pinned on the totally untried 7-litre cars, later referred to as Mark IIs, a pair being entered for the 24-hours. They were joined at the Sarthe by four other Fords, two of which were practised with 5.3-litre engines. The results were every bit as bad as the previous year, all the Fords retiring within seven hours, from a variety of causes. The Colotti gearboxes could no longer be blamed, as they had been replaced in the smaller engined cars by ZF units, and in the Mark IIs by Ford's own T-44 transaxle.

The first true "privateer" GT40 had been delivered on May 13, 1965, but deliveries did not re-commence until August of that year, by which time all the classic races were long over so it was not until 1966 that privately entered GT40s arrived in quantity on the track.

1966 saw the powers-that-be at Ford in no doubt as to where their efforts were to be concentrated, the Mark II being chosen to redeem Ford's rather tarnished image. This time, there were to be no mistakes, and Henry Ford II's famous edict "Win – or else" let everyone know just how seriously Ford were taking the whole affair. The season opened with the Daytona Continental, extended to be of full 24-hours duration; five well prepared Mk IIs were there at the start, and four of them were still running at the end, in first, second, third and fifth positions. The highest placed small-block GT40 managed 14th position, suggesting that Ford had been correct in putting the emphasis on the Mk II programme.

The next race contested by the Mark IIs was at Sebring, where the team of Ken Miles and Lloyd Ruby repeated their Daytona success, this time at the wheel of the open-bodied Mark II, the X-1. In 12th place was an experimental Mk II, using a two-speed semi-automatic gearbox. Sebring had seen the debut of the Alan Mann-developed alloy-bodied GT40s, which proved commendably fast, but could not stand the pace set by the Mark IIs. Following Sebring, the Mark IIs were stripped and rebuilt for Le Mans, the only intervening appearances of these cars being two examples at the Le Mans test days, where one was written off, and at Spa, where the survivor of the pair was entrusted to Alan Mann Racing. It managed second place behind a works Ferrari, but was hard pressed throughout the race by the Essex Wire GT40 of Skip Scott and Peter Revson.

The weekend of June 18th and 19th 1966, saw the running of the 34th *Grand Prix d'Endurance* at Le Mans, the race being attended by "The Deuce", Henry Ford II himself, who intended that his visit to the race should naturally be rounded off by the sight of his cars winning. In an attempt to ensure that he would not be disappointed, and that they would keep their jobs, his men sought to enter no fewer than *fifteen* Mark IIs for the event! Such steamroller tactics were resisted by the race organisers, the ACO, who allocated eight entries to

the works teams. Backed by five GT40s, the Mark IIs set out to dominate the race, outpacing works Ferraris in a way never before seen at the Sarthe. The weekend ended happily for Ford, the Mark IIs taking the first three places, although all the 289-powered GT40s retired.

Their goal achieved, Ford could have pulled out of racing, but instead chose to defend their position as Le Mans winners the following season. As in 1966, the season's opening race was at Daytona, where Ford expected a repeat win with their six Mark IIs. They were to be cruelly disappointed, for, one by one, the six succumbed to gearbox maladies, a badly heat-treated shaft in each gearbox causing their downfall. Eventually, two good spares were located, and these were fitted to the best placed cars, as they struggled towards the finish, miles behind the trio of Ferraris which dominated the race. For the next event, at Sebring, only a single Mark II was entered, and this was only as back-up to the single Mark IV, which had been developed from the previous year's J-car prototype. The Mark IV won, after the transmission on its principal rival, a Chaparral 2F, expired. The Mark II was in a secure second place when its camshaft broke, and it sat out the remaining laps of the race in its pit. Despite not finishing, it had covered a greater distance than the third place Porsche 910, so remained in second position at the end.

There was to be no more factory participation until Le Mans, so the other European races were left to privately entered GT40s to wave the Ford flag. Easily the most effective were the JW-developed Mirages, which scored an impressive win at Spa where driver Jackie Ickx excelled on the rain-soaked track. Ford had not been at all interested in the Mirage, until the Spa win brought championship points into question but, alas for Ford, the car had been entered as a Mirage, and the points went to

Mirage, not to Ford.

The Le Mans line-up for 1967 was no less impressive than had been the previous year's, although emphasis had moved away from the GT40 towards the Mark IV, which formed the main portion of the Ford arsenal, four such cars being entered. The trusty Mark II, in its updated IIB form, acted as back-up, three cars being in the line-up; the small-block brigade was led by a pair of Mirages with 305 CID engines, from three 289-engined GT40s. The Ford/Ferrari struggle lasted right to the end, with two Mark IVs being the only Fords to finish, albeit in first and fourth places. The result could have been even better, but two Mark IIs and a Mark IV were eliminated in a single accident at the Esses, fortunately without injury to any of the drivers. The point had been well and truly made, and Ford, with two Le Mans victories to their credit, were happy to pull out of sports car racing, particularly as an engine capacity limit was looming.

Although the works had lost interest, JW Automotive still saw life in the old GT40, and the engine size limit of 5-litres, which was imposed for 1968 on, would not affect the car. Consequently, one of the Mirages was converted to a GT40, and a brand-new GT40 built as its team-mate. The opposition was no longer Ferrari who, badly affected by the capacity limit, had withdrawn at the same time as Ford; this time the adversary was Porsche, with both Matra and Alpine-Renault expected to provide additional stiff competition. Daytona once more marked the season's opening, and the GT40s were really at home on its long straight, and its banked curves. They qualified fastest and led easily until they were both sidelined by gearbox troubles, caused by unexpected loads imposed by the adoption of larger tyres. On to Sebring, where again the cars were in their element, until they once more retired, one having spun and the other having hit a wayward

Rambler Javelin.

Things were looking bleak for the Gulf-sponsored cars, but their fortunes were to improve with the return to Europe, victories being gained at Brands Hatch and Monza, whilst Ickx showed once more his mastery of the GT40 in the rain, by repeating his 1967 victory at Spa. Prior to Le Mans, which had been postponed until September due to political unrest in France, JW GT40s went over to the USA to take the first two places at Watkins Glen. Entering the final round, at Le Mans, both Ford and Porsche could win the championship, the outcome of the race being decisive. Despite losing both Ickx and Redman to injuries, JW's GT40s outlasted the Porsches, the Rodriguez/Bianchi car being the only surviving GT40, in a secure first place. 1968 thus ended well for the GT40, with both Le Mans and the championship to its credit.

The GT40's age was beginning to tell as it moved into its sixth season, 1969, and the car was looking decidedly heavy and cumbersome by the standards of the day. JW Automotive decided to use it only as a stop-gap, until their Mirage M2/300 (which had nothing in common with the GT40-based Mirage) could be sufficiently developed to enter the fray. Thus the Gulf GT40s took part in only four events in 1969, at Daytona, Sebring, Brands Hatch and Le Mans. At Daytona they led until their retirement, following the earlier retirement of the works Porsche team: the race was to provide the Lola T-70 with its only significant victory. At Sebring the opposition was joined by Ferrari, whose new 312P very nearly won, but in a battle of attrition it was narrowly beaten by the Ickx/Oliver GT40. At Brands Hatch in the BOAC 500 race, the Gulf GT40 could manage no better than 5th, although that was good enough to

be a class victory. JW kept their GT40s away from the other European races, but the German team of *Deutsche Auto Zeitung* showed that the GT40 was still the best production sports car around by taking class wins at both the Nurburgring and Monza.

Once more attention was focused on Le Mans, and it was obvious that this was to be no easy run for the GT40s: Porsche were present with an extensive team, comprising four of the 3-litre 908s and two of the fearsome 4.5-litre 917s. On paper, the Gulf GT40s stood no chance, for they had to contend with a brace of very fast Ferraris too. The race went into the history books as the most exciting long-distance race ever, with the result being in doubt right up to the chequered flag. The largely untried Porsches fell by the wayside, until it came to one GT40, driven by Ickx, fighting a wheel to wheel battle with the sole remaining Porsche 908, with Hans Herrmann at the controls. Ickx described his drive in the book *My Greatest Race* – the way he assessed the situation and outdrove the Porsche to snatch victory by some hundred yards after

24 hours of racing is the stuff of which legends are made. The GT40 at the centre of the action was none other than 1075, which had won the previous year, to become the first (and, so far, the only) car ever to win twice at Le Mans.

So ended the GT40's real racing career. It would be fielded in a desultory fashion by private entrants during the next two years, but its 1969 season was effectively its last, and certainly its finest.

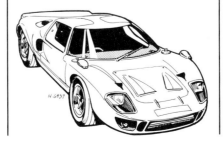

EVOLUTION

The first prototype was number **101,** being completed in April 1964. Its first foray onto the racetrack proved to be its last, as it was written off at the Le Mans test days later that month. Its sister car **102** narrowly avoided the same fate at the same event, but survived to make the marque's first entry into an actual race, the Nurburgring 1000km. By that time it had been rebuilt with a spoiler across the tail, and a revised nose section with relocated driving lights. Eventually it was written off during testing at Monza when, with Sir John Whitmore at the wheel, it left the track when the throttle stuck open.

103 was identical to 102 when it first appeared at Le Mans in 1964. It was rebuilt by Shelby American to incorporate the interim 1965 front-end, and repositioned rear-mounted oil-coolers. **104** also raced initially at Le Mans, for Ford Advanced Vehicles, before eventually receiving the same modifications as 103, at Shelby American.

105 was externally similar to 103 when built, but became the first car to receive the 289 engine, when the 255 was in short supply. The car underwent many modifications during its long career as an FAV development vehicle. Both **106** and **107** were built with 427 CID, 7-litre engines, and

extended nose sections for Le Mans in 1965. What happened to them subsequently is not known, but it is possible that one of them was cut in two so that the rear part could be used as a rig to hold the 427 for dynamometer tests. In this form it appeared in a Timken advertisement.

108 and **109** were built as roadsters, rarely being raced, but used by Shelby for experimental purposes. Contrary to earlier reports, these cars were never rebuilt as coupes, and still exist as open cars in the USA. 109 now has a quad-cam Indy engine and a ZF gearbox.

110 was an alloy chassis, sent to Bruce McLaren at his Feltham premises, to be completed as the X-1 roadster, basically an open-topped version of 106 and 107. It was later rebuilt, still on the alloy chassis, as an open-topped Mark IIA.

The final two prototypes were **111** and **112,** which were both built as roadsters for Ford Advanced Vehicles. 111 was damaged at the 1965 Targa Florio; what happened to it subsequently has not been recorded. 112 was later rebodied as a standard coupe.

The initial production chassis, **1000,** was used at first only to test the fit of body panels intended for other cars. Completed in its own right in January 1966, it was shipped to the Comstock team for use in that year's Sebring 12-hour race; sadly, it was totally destroyed there in the tragic accident which took the life of Canadian Bob McLean. **1001** started out as a 1965 exhibition vehicle, posing as a Shelby prototype. It returned to the works to be brought up to 1966 specification, with fuel crossover system and, later, rear brake ducts. Externally it could be identified by the air-scoop on the driver's door. F English Ltd, of Bournemouth, received the first GT40 to race in private hands; their car, **1002,** was finished in powder blue, and fitted with a luggage grid. It was modified many times during its long career,

but could usually be identified by its registration number, FEL 1C.

1003 was to 1965 specification for Ford France, but was prepared by Shelby American for its first outing, at the Nurburgring. Both **1004** and **1005** were to identical 1965 specification, with blue interior trim, when sent to Shelby for completion. **1006** was the first car to have the definitive nose section, in June 1965: it was badly damaged at Monza, and later rebuilt with alloy panels from AMGT2. **1007** was the last car to feature the row of aeroflow vents in the roof. It was exhibited at the Monza Show before taking up its racing career with Ford France. **1008** was built to standard specification but, following Ford's 1966 Le Mans victory, was turned into a replica of the winning Mark II. After the first Gulf-JW victory, it was again rebodied, as a replica of Gulf car 1075. The first car to be delivered in kit form was **1009,** for Peter Sutcliffe. It was wrecked at Kyalami in November 1968, the remains eventually being rebuilt; in the meantime, a leftover Mark II chassis had formed the basis for a second '1009', built for owner Malcolm Guthrie by Alan Mann Racing. **1010** was delivered to Essex Wire late in 1965; during testing it was wrecked and rebuilt around a replacement chassis in 1966.

The first production Mark IIs were **1011** and **1012,** delivered to Shelby in August 1965 for completion in the USA. The fortunes and specifications of individual Mark IIs have so far proved difficult to document, as all but the first two are reputed to have been delivered without chassis plates. Most Mark IIs still survive, and carry serials, but these are not thought to be originals, and may well be on the wrong cars. Other Mark IIs were **1015, 1016, 1031, 1032, 1047,** and **1046,** the latter believed to be the 1966 Le Mans winner. Three other chassis, **XGT1, XGT2** and **XGT3,** went from Alan Mann to Shelby American for completion as Mark IIs.

Production of road cars began with **1013**, which had chassis underseal and a 2-plate clutch, together with grilles fitted into various scoops. It carried registration OVX 355D when tested by the press in 1966. **1014** was built to racing specification for Karl Richardson, whilst the next racer, **1017**, was supplied in kit form and unpainted to F English Ltd, who used it for Spa and Le Mans in 1966. **1018** had a show finish and maroon paintwork when sent to Shelby in November 1965 for an American customer. Another unpainted car was **1019**, which had a revised fuel system and Halibrand wheels when collected by Alan Mann Racing. **1020** left the factory in midnight blue show finish, but was repainted white by new owners Ford France. **1021** was sold to Nick Cussons, later going to Colin Crabbe, who fitted its roof with an enormous bulge to accommodate tall drivers.

1022 wore Gipsy Red paintwork on delivery to Nick Cuthbert for Eric Liddell to drive. **1023, 1024, 1025, 1030, 1035** and **1036** were all engineless and unpainted when they left Slough. The first of them went to Alan Mann, and the remainder to Shelby, who returned all except **1024** to Britain, due to registration problems. **1026** was a standard racer for Essex Wire; it was fitted with quick-lift jacking points at the front. **1027**, which was exhibited at the Brussels Show, was used as a camera car for the filming of *Grand Prix*; it now has a four-cam engine. **1028** had leather trim and air-conditioning when delivered as a road car. **1029** was Scuderia Bear's ill-fated racer, finished in silver with stripes in red, white and blue. When **1033** left the works it was without trim, being sent to Graber for completion as a luxurious special for the Geneva Show in 1966; it was later converted to a race car for ASA ESCA.

1034, a pine green road car, had such extras as a heated screen, and reversing lights. Comstock's second racer was **1037**, featuring a deeper than usual radiator intake, as had been used on 1000. **1038** had Le Mans gear ratios fitted when despatched to Essex Wire in April 1966. Scuderia Filipinetti's two GT40s were **1039** and **1040**, both in Signal Red, with a white fore and aft stripe. Belgian Jean Blaton, better known under the pseudonym "Beurlys", bought **1041**, which was painted in silver with Belgian Racing stripes; a Cleveland engine was fitted. Scuderia Brescia Corse took two cars, their second being **1042**, in white, with red, white and green sill stripes and FAV wheels in place of the usual Borranis.

1043, a road car sold in the USA via Shelby American, had air-conditioning, as had **1044**, which, with its host of electrical extras including Sony micro TV, was certainly the most comprehensively equipped GT40. **1045** was a road car for Girling Ltd, whilst **1048** became Brescia Corse's first racer. It was the last GT40 ever to race at Le Mans, in the 1971 3-hour race, for which it was fitted with a cut-away rear body section. When built it had red paintwork, rear brake ducts and both Borrani and FAV wheels. Although technically a road car, **1049** had a race-tuned engine and a competition clutch installed at the request of its first owner, Gulf Oil's vice-president, Grady Davis. General Motors bought **1050**, an air-conditioned road car and used it to develop rear-mounted radiator installations for mid-engined Corvette prototypes; it was unusual in being fitted with a single Holley carburettor in place of the more common Webers. **1051** to **1072** were all road cars, with Borrani wheels, 289 Weber-carburetted engines and 2-plate clutches; most were sold in the USA via Ford Division, and differed mainly in their colours, although **1072** received Mark III windows at its customer's request.

1073 was a bare chassis, delivered to Terry Drury in November 1967, for completion by him. Race car production recommenced with **1074**, converted from Mirage M10003 to Gulf specification, which included a lightweight roof with inner panel in aluminium, carbon-fibre reinforced body panels, a lightweight chassis and an aluminium fully ducted spare wheel cover. Both **1075** and **1076** were built to the same Gulf specification, being completed in January and September, 1968, respectively. The next race cars were basically to the same standard, although some lacked the fuel crossover system used on Gulf cars. Yamaha bought **1077**, painted yellow with a white stripe, and **1078** went to Geoffrey Edwards to race under the Strathaven banner, in that team's Borneo Green livery. **1079**, in yellow finish, went to Jean Blaton; it was written off at Le Mans in 1968, but the remains have eventually been rebuilt, and fitted with a Peugeot four cylinder engine! Firestone anti-surge foam was put into the fuel tanks of white painted **1080**, delivered to A F Pires in Portugal. IGFA/*Deutsche Auto Zeitung* raced **1081** with considerable success in 1969; it was converted for road use in Germany, and had to wear hubcaps to comply with German regulations.

1082 raced as a Ford France entry in 1969, but was actually owned by Michel Martin. The final car completed by JW was **1083**, despatched to the Colegio Arte & Instruccao Team in Brazil during October 1969. **1084** was a 1968 rebuild of 1004, to Gulf standards, whilst **1085** was a bare chassis sold to Malcolm Guthrie in March 1969; it currently nears completion in the USA. **1086** was a leftover chassis which was commenced in 1971 but which is still unfinished.

Only two Alan Mann chassis received alloy bodywork, these being **AMGT1**, demolished while being driven "without the owner's consent", and **AMGT2**, which, its alloy panels replaced by fibreglass, was driven so well by Paul Hawkins in the late 'sixties.

None of the Mark IIIs had competition careers, all being used solely as road cars. **1101** was the left-hand-drive prototype, built up from modified Mark I parts; it was later rebuilt to full Mark III standards, with a 302 hydraulic-lifter engine. Blue painted **1102,** now in the National Motor Museum at Beaulieu, received a 289 Holley carburetted engine, as did **1105** and **1104,** which also received air-conditioning. **1103** had a solid-lifter 302, as used in **1107,** the last Mark III completed, but **1106** was fitted with an hydraulic-lifter 302 and Autolite carburettor.

SPECIFICATION

Type designation		Ford GT, GT40, Mark II, Mark III, Mirage.

Chassis numbers

Prototypes:	(1964/5)	GT/101 to 112.
GT40 Race cars:	(1965)	GT40P/1001 to 1010, 1014, 1017 to 1025, 1030.
	(1966)	GT40P/1000, 1026, 1027, 1029, 1035 to 1041, 1048.
	(1967)	GT40P/1042, 1073.
	(1968)	GT40P/1074 to 1079, 1084.
	(1969)	GT40P/1080 to 1083, 1085.
	(1971)	GT40P/1086.
GT40 Road cars:	(1965)	GT40P/1013.
	(1966)	GT40P/1028, 1033, 1034, 1043 to 1045, 1049 to 1067.
	(1967)	GT40P/1068 to 1072.
Mark II:	(1965)	GT40P/1011, 1012, 1015, 1016, 1031, 1032.
	(1966)	GT40P/1046, 1047.
Mark III:	(1967)	GT40M3/1101, 1102.
	(1968)	GT40M3/1104 to 1106.
	(1969)	GT40M3/1103, 1107.
Mirage:	(1967)	M1/10001 to 10003.
Alan Mann cars:	(1966)	AMGT/1 & 2 (lightweight GT40), XGT1, 2 & 3.
	(1969)	GT40P/1009.

The dates shown above are those when the chassis or the complete car, as appropriate, left Ford Advanced Vehicles and JW Automotive Engineering.

Built by	Chassis built by Abbey Panels*, Coventry, and completed by Ford Advanced Vehicles Ltd. and its successor, JW Automotive Engineering Ltd. Prototypes GT/106 and 107 were completed by Kar Kraft, at Dearborn; Mark IIs were completed at Shelby American, Los Angeles, California. Alan Mann Cars were built at Byfleet, Surrey, from chassis obtained direct from Abbey Panels, although the Mark IIs went to Shelby American for completion.

Engine

	1964 GT Prototype	1966 Mk IIA	1966 GT40	1969 Gulf GT40
Block:	Aluminium	Cast iron	Cast iron	Cast iron
Heads:	Aluminium	Aluminium	Cast iron	Aluminium

	1964 GT Prototype	1966 Mk IIA	1966 GT40	1969 Gulf GT40
Cylinders (90° V8)				
Bore:	3.76in/95.5mm	4.24in/107.5mm	4.00in/101.6mm	4.00in/101.6mm
Stroke:	2.87in/72.9mm	3.78in/96.1mm	2.87in/72.9mm	3.00in/76.2mm
Capacity:	255CID/4181cc	427CID/6982cc	289CID/4728cc	302CID/4942cc
Bhp/rpm:	350/7200	485/6200	390/7000	425/6000
Torque/rpm:	275/5600	475/3200-3600	325/5000	396/4750
Compression ratio:	12.5:1	10.5:1	12.5:1	10.6:1
Camshafts (all models):	1, central, with pushrod overhead valves.			
Carburettors:	4-Weber 48IDA	1-Holley 4V	4-Weber 48IDA	4-Weber 48IDA
Lubrication:	Dry sump	Dry sump	Wet sump	Wet sump
Transmission				
Clutch:	Borg & Beck 7$\frac{1}{4}$in	Long 10in,2-plate	Borg & Beck 7$\frac{1}{4}$in	Borg & Beck 7$\frac{1}{4}$in
Gearbox				
Make:	Colotti	Ford T-44	ZF-5DS-25	ZF-5DS-25
Type:	4-speed	4-speed synchro	5-speed synchro	5-speed synchro
Ratios - I:	2.50	2.22	2.42	2.23
II:	1.70	1.43	1.47	1.53
III:	1.29	1.19	1.09	1.21
IV:	1.00	1.00	0.96	1.00
V:	–	–	0.85	0.81
Final drive:	3.09	2.77 (effective)	4.22 (sprint)	3.20 (Enduro)
Mph/1000rpm (in top):	28.9	31.5	22.0	31.5
Wheelbase	7ft 11in	7ft 11in	7ft 11in	7ft 11in
Track				
Front:	4ft 6in	4ft 9in	4ft 6in	4ft 9$\frac{1}{2}$in
Rear:	4ft 6in	4ft 8in	4ft 6in	4ft 10$\frac{1}{2}$in
Length	158.5in	163in	164.5in	164.5in
Width	70in	70in	70in	75in
Height	40.5in	40.5in	40.5in	40.5in
Suspension				
Front:	Independent; double A-frames, coil springs, magnesium uprights, anti-roll bar.			
Rear:	Independent; double trailing links from rear bulkhead, lower inverted A-frame, upper transverse link, coil springs, anti-roll bar.			
Chassis (all models):	Mid-engined, semi-monocoque, in 0.024in/0.028in sheet steel, with steel square-tube extensions to front and rear body supports.			
Bodywork (all models):	Fibreglass front and rear detachable covers, doors and sills, with carbon fibre reinforcement on Gulf cars. Roof in steel.			
Steering (rack and pinion)				
Ratio:	14:1	16:1	14:1	–
Turns lock-to-lock:	–	2.25	2.8	–
Turning circle:	–	34ft	37ft	–

	1964 GT Prototype	1966 Mk IIA	1966 GT40	1969 Gulf GT40
Brakes (Discs)				
Type:	Girling, solid	Ford, ventilated	Girling, solid	Girling, ventilated
Diameter:	11.56in	11.56in	11.56in	11.95in
Thickness:	0.5in	0.775in	0.5in	0.75in
Wheels				
Type:	Borrani, wire	Halibrand, alloy	Borrani, wire	Aeroplane & Motor, alloy
Size (front):	6½inx15in	8inx15in	6inx15in	10inx15in
Size (rear):	8inx15in	12inx15in	9inx15in	14inx15in
Tyres				
Front:	5.50x15	9.75x15	5.50x15	475/10.30x15
Rear:	7.25x15	12.80x15	7.00x15	600/13.50x15
Fuel capacity (Imp/US gal):	30.5/37	35/42	30.5/37	30.5/37
Electrical system (typical):	Alternator, 12volt	052 amps; Battery,	53 ampere/hour	
Performance				
0-100mph:	9 secs	8 secs	9 secs	8 secs
Max. speed:	197mph	215mph	195mph	210mph
Weight (at Le Mans scrutineering) Chassis number (weight in pounds):	102 (2308)	1046 (2670)	1017 (2440)	1075 (2469)

* The exact number of chassis produced by Abbey Panels is not known, as their records were destroyed in a fire. When J.W.
Automotive terminated production, several chassis remained unused, and some of these have since been used to manufacture new cars or rebuild others. New cars are variously un-numbered and incorrectly numbered, making determination of total production difficult. All cars listed above, with the exception of 1101, and 1104 to 1106, were right-hand-drive. Some left-hand-drive GT40s have been built on previously unused Mark III chassis.

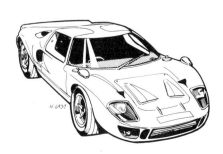

ROAD TESTS

CAR and DRIVER ROAD TEST

FORD MARK III

The workmanship and most of the hardware in this, the most costly Ford
of all, are miserably below the standards of the meanest Falcon.

PHOTOGRAPHY: JOHN HEARST

In theory, the Ford Mk. III should be the world's most desirable enthusiast's car. In theory, the Mk. III is a streetworthy replica of Ford's GT 40—derivatives of which have won Le Mans and the World Sports Car Manufacturers Championship. In theory, this $18,500 car ought to be worth $1500 less than twenty thousand bucks.

In practice, those theories come apart at the seams—like the Mk. III we tested, which was barely 2600 miles old.

To be fair, Ford's representatives assured us that our test car was one of the first Mk. IIIs built and that all our objections would be stilled when the Mk. III program gets rolling. We certainly hope so.

But the fact remains that the workmanship and most of the hardware in this, the most costly Ford of all, are miserably below the standards of the meanest Falcon.

Most of what's wrong with the Mk. III happened in the translation from racer to street machine. We've driven the original GT 40 (C/D, November '65) and the big Mk. II (C/D, April '67), and we loved them both. The Mk. III is like a wholly different car.

In the first place, it's about as reliable as a two-dollar watch. The electrical system was out to lunch half the time. One driving light didn't work, a parking light had fallen out, the brake-system warning light glowed ominously all the time (the Ford people swore the brakes were okay), and everything except the ignition circuit would cut out at unpredictable moments— then mysteriously cure itself. A control stalk seemed to be connected to the high voltage side of the coil, zapping anybody who tried to use the horn. The shoulder harness inertia reels didn't work, leaving the interior cluttered with yards of useless safety belting. The right-hand door kept flying open. The seat upholstery was coming unglued. The windshield adhesive was smeared all over the dashboard. The transmission and clutch linkages were hope-

(continued)

Prior experience with GT 40s
and Mk. IIs had prepared
us to be enthralled with the
street version, but as we got
to know the Mk. III . . .

lessly fouled up. The fuel tank changeover tap was stuck, leaving us with only half of the fuel supply —which, at seven miles per, didn't last very long.

All these are simple quality control problems—and simply unpardonable. At least *we* wouldn't be in a very forgiving mood if we'd just shelled out $18,500 for the car, would *you*?

There are also several design flaws, most of them easily rectified, but we couldn't help wondering why no one had given them much thought before. As a typical example, the fuel line passes so close to the hot engine that vapor lock is never more than a few degrees away. Or: there's so much padding on the floor that the already scarce foot room is even more restricted. And the padding is inadequately

secured to the floor, so that it gets all wadded up under the pedals. Enough?

Economy measures are rampant, despite the fact that the Mk. III costs some $2000 more than the GT 40 race cars. The Mk. III's seats are modified British Restall units that retail for about $60, are miserably uncomfortable for anyone much over five-ten, and adjust fore and aft only with considerable difficulty. In the race cars, the seats—marvelously comfortable—are fixed, and the pedals are moveable. The Mk. III's seats contribute nothing; their only virtue is that they're obviously cheaper than the race car's assembly. Many of the other proprietary components are low-cost bits and pieces from British economy sedans, and seem decidedly second-rate when applied to a hyper-expensive

Grand Touring machine like this.

Our prior experience with GT 40s and Mk. IIs had prepared us to be enthralled with the street version, but as we got to know the Mk. III, and more and more imperfections reared their shoddy heads, our esteem plummeted. Yet, somehow, the car that the Mk. III was intended to be still shone through and thrilled us. Underneath, it's still a thoroughbred.

The Mk. III is built by J.W. Automotive Engineering, Ltd. The initials stand for ex-team manager (for Ford and Aston Martin) John Wyer, and Ford distributor (in England) John Willment. J.W. Automotive Engineering took over the now-defunct Ford Advanced Vehicles facility at Slough, and sells completed Mk. IIIs to Ford, as well as doing sub-contract work on the racing

. . . and more and more imperfections reared their shoddy heads. our esteem plummeted. Yet somehow, the car that the Mk. III was intended to be shone through and thrilled us. Underneath, it's still a thoroughbred.

A basically intelligent interior is spoiled by poor seats and hardware.

A quad lighting system replaces the race car's square Cibie units.

Carburetor air is drawn into plenum chamber under the rear window.

cars. The GT 40s and Mk. IIIs are distributed in this country by Carroll Shelby's organization. The Mk. IIIs are sold through Ford High-Performance Dealers, like New York's Gotham Ford, which, through Gotham's Bill Kolb, Jr., is where we borrowed our test car.

There are few basic differences between the race cars and the Mk. III. The sheet steel body/chassis center hull-section is retained, although the spaces between double-skinned sections are filled with a polyurethane foam that absorbs noise, heat, and—for safety—energy. In the race cars, the side pontoons that comprise the main structural members of the chassis are filled with two 18.5-gallon rubber fuel bladders. In the Mk. IIIs, a pair of smaller, 13.8-gallon baffled aluminum tanks are surrounded with a two-inch-thick layer of polyurethane foam to lessen fire hazard in case of a crash.

The front and rear body sections are fiberglass, and are of remarkably good quality. The nose has been restyled to move the headlights up to legal height for street use and to allow the use of sealed beams instead of the generally illegal (in the U.S.) square Cibie headlights. The sealed beams are paired with a set of Marchal driving lights and set under plexiglass fairings, both also illegal in several states. The rear section has been lengthened eight inches to provide a very small (six cubic feet) luggage "locker" over the transaxle and muffler system. The small, lockable front compartment is completely filled by the spare tire. The altered body shape results in a steeper approach angle, but a flatter departure angle, and the tail scrapes on the ground at fairly mild changes of road angle.

The Mk. III's engine is the same high-performance, 306-horsepower, 289 cu. in. V-8 installed in the Shelby American GT 350s (complete with exhaust emission control), not the 385-hp, Weber-carbureted 289s used in the GT 40s that won the World Manufacturers Championship for Ford last year, and not the 427 cu. in. NASCAR-type engines used

(Text continued on page 92; Specifications overleaf)

FORD GT 40 MK. III

Importer: Shelby American Inc.
6501 West Imperial Highway
Los Angeles, Calif.

Number of dealers in U.S.: 90

Vehicle type: Mid-engine, rear-wheel-drive, 2-passenger GT car, fiberglass body on a stressed steel hull and roof

Price as tested: $18,500.00
(Manufacturer's suggested retail price, plus Federal excise tax, dealer preparation and delivery charges; does not include state and local taxes, license or freight charges)

Options on test car: None

ENGINE
Type: Water-cooled V-8, cast iron block and heads, 5 main bearings
Bore x stroke . . . . 4.00 x 2.87 in, 101.7 x 72.9 mm
Displacement . . . . 289 cu in, 4737 cc
Compression ratio . . . . 10.5 to one
Carburetion . . . . 1 x 4-bbl Holley
Valve gear . . . . Pushrod-operated overhead valves, mechanical lifters
Power (SAE) . . . . 306 bhp @ 6000 rpm
Torque (SAE) . . . . 329 lbs/ft @ 4200 rpm
Specific power output . . . . 1.06 bhp/cu in, 64.6 bhp/liter
Max. recommended engine speed . . . 6200 rpm

DRIVE TRAIN
Transmission . . . . 5-speed, all-synchro
Clutch diameter . . . . 8.5 in (two-plate)
Final drive ratio . . . . 4.22 to one

Gear	Ratio	Mph/1000 rpm	Max. test speed
I	2.42	7.7	48 mph (6200 rpm)
II	1.47	12.9	80 mph (6200 rpm)
III	1.09	17.6	109 mph (6200 rpm)
IV	0.96	20.0	124 mph (6200 rpm)
V/OD	0.85	22.7	136 mph (6000 rpm)

DIMENSIONS AND CAPACITIES
Wheelbase . . . . 95.3 in
Track . . . . . . F: 55.2 in, R: 55.2 in
Length . . . . 169.0 in
Width . . . . 70.0 in
Height . . . . 41.0 in
Ground clearance . . . . 5.25 in
Curb weight . . . . 2340 lbs
Test weight . . . . 2706 lbs
Weight distribution, F/R 45/55%
Lbs/bhp (test weight) 8.85
Battery capacity . . . . 12 volts 60 amp/hr
Alternator capacity . . . . 504 watts
Fuel capacity . . . . 27.6 gal
Oil capacity . . . . 9.5 qts

SUSPENSION
F: Ind., unequal length wishbones, coil springs, anti-sway bar
R: Ind., triangulated lower control arm, single strut upper control arm, two trailing arms, coil springs, anti-sway bar

STEERING
Type . . . . Rack and pinion
Turns lock-to-lock 2.5
Turning circle . . . . 32.0 ft

BRAKES
F: Girling 11.5-in solid discs
R: Girling 11.2-in solid discs
Swept area . . . . 240 sq in

WHEELS AND TIRES
Wheel size and type . . . .
F: 6½L x 15-in, alloy-rim Borrani knock-off wire wheels
R: 8L x 15-in, alloy-rim Borrani knock-off wire wheels
Tire make, size and type . . . . :
F: Goodyear 5.00/8.90-15 racing (wet weather)
R: Goodyear 7.00-15 racing (wet weather)
Test inflation pressures . . F: 28 psi, R: 32 psi
Tire load rating . . . F: 1100 lbs per tire @ 24 psi
R: 1600 lbs per tire @ 24 psi

PERFORMANCE
Zero to	Seconds
30 mph	1.6
40 mph	2.3
50 mph	3.8
60 mph	5.1
70 mph	6.6
80 mph	8.2
90 mph	10.2
100 mph	12.7

Standing ¼-mile . . . . 13.8 sec @ 104.8 mph
80-0 mph . . . . 242 ft (.88 G)
Fuel mileage . . . . 7-10 mpg on premium fuel
Cruising range . . . . 193-276 mi

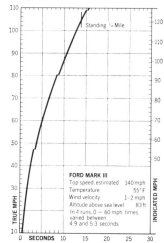

FORD MARK III
Top speed, estimated 140 mph
Temperature 55°F
Wind velocity 1-2 mph
Altitude above sea level 83 ft
In 4 runs, 0 — 60 mph times varied between 4.9 and 5.3 seconds

CHECK LIST

ENGINE
Starting . . . . Poor
Response . . . . Excellent
Vibration . . . . Very Good
Noise . . . . Very Good

DRIVE TRAIN
Shift linkage . . . . Unacceptable
Synchro action . . . . Very Good
Clutch smoothness . . . . Unacceptable
Drive train noise . . . . Good

STEERING
Effort . . . . Excellent
Response . . . . Excellent
Road feel . . . . Excellent
Kickback . . . . Fair

SUSPENSION
Ride comfort . . . . Good
Roll resistance . . . . Excellent
Pitch control . . . . Excellent
Harshness control . . . . Fair

HANDLING
Directional control . . . . Excellent
Predictability . . . . Excellent
Evasive maneuverability . . . . Excellent
Resistance to sidewinds . . . . Excellent

BRAKES
Pedal pressure . . . . Excellent
Response . . . . Excellent
Fade resistance . . . . Excellent
Directional stability . . . . Fair

CONTROLS
Wheel position . . . . Poor
Pedal position . . . . Fair
Gearshift position . . . . Poor
Relationship . . . . Fair
Small controls . . . . Poor

INTERIOR
Ease of entry/exit . . . . 'Unacceptable
Noise level (cruising) . . . . Fair
Front seating comfort . . . . Poor
Front leg room . . . . Fair
Front head room . . . . Poor
Front hip/shoulder room . . . . Poor
Instrument comprehensiveness . . . Excellent
Instrument legibility . . . . Excellent

VISION
Forward . . . . Good
Front quarter . . . . Good
Side . . . . Very Good
Rear quarter . . . . Poor
Rear . . . . Fair

WEATHER PROTECTION
Heater/defroster . . . . Fair
Ventilation . . . . Good
Air conditioner . . . . —
Weather sealing . . . . Good

CONSTRUCTION QUALITY
Sheet metal/fiberglass . . . . Very Good
Paint . . . . Very Good
Chrome . . . . Very Good
Upholstery . . . . Poor
Padding . . . . Good
Hardware . . . . Poor

GENERAL
Headlight illumination . . . . Excellent
Parking and signal lights . . . . Good
Wiper effectiveness . . . . Very Good
Service accessibility . . . . Good
Trunk space . . . . Poor
Interior storage space . . . . Fair
Bumper protection . . . . Poor

2

HAPPINESS IS . . . *HAVING FUN WITH A*
Le MANS WINNER

Driving the JW Automotive Engineering's winning Ford GT40 at Silverstone enabled Innes Ireland to appreciate the very considerable amount of development work done on the car since he drove some of the early models. Here he describes some of the changes and how the car handles today.

by Innes Ireland

WHEN I first spoke to John Wyer, of JW Automotive Engineering Ltd, and asked him if I could have a canter round Silverstone in his Le Mans winning GT40 he immediately said "Yes, we would be delighted—we'll let you know when it can be arranged." At the time of asking the car had not returned from the Paris Motor Show where it was on display, but was due back in a few days.

It then transpired that there was some difficulty since the car was not registered in this country, and during the time of its stay in England it would be in bond. However, through the good offices of HM Customs and Excise at Berkshire House in Maidenhead, and with Mr. King's help in particular, we were allowed to take it out for a day.

Martin Lewis and I set off in my London-Sydney Mercedes-Benz, for it was our intention to calibrate the instruments through the medium of a fifth wheel. The drive up the M1 was misery, for it was damp and foggy, and when we arrived at Silverstone the whole circuit was clad in a nasty, claggy blanket of Scotch mist.

I was anxious to get on the circuit with the car, which had already been rolled out of the JW Engineering transporter and was being warmed up. Having done a considerable amount of development driving on the GT40 in the early days, I could barely contain my curiosity to find out about handling improvements. But first it was necessary to study the cockpit layout and find out about the car itself.

The first thing to bear in mind is that every racing car is an individual, and its individuality stems from the chaps that are going to drive it. During the season this particular car has been driven by several different people and its particular character is really a bit of each one of them, culminating with the efforts of Pedro Rodriguez and Lucien Bianchi who drove it to victory in Les Vingt-Quatre Heures du Mans, 1968.

To take a quick look at the car's history this year, it won the BOAC 500 at Brands Hatch with Ickx and Redman, who also drove it to victory at Spa. The other major victory it scored was at Watkins Glen when Ickx and Bianchi were the drivers. It competed at Daytona where the gearbox broke, Sebring where Redman spun it and burned out the clutch and Monza where, first of all, the exhaust system broke and then Redman spun it and damaged the bodywork which finally put the car out of the race. It could have continued in fact, but so much time had been lost that it wasn't worth it.

Memories of Le Mans flooded back to me as I climbed into the car. The bodywork was still in the grimy, travel-stained, oil-smeared state in which it drove into the winner's circle, and I could almost smell the slightly stale aroma of sweat from the driver's seat. There were the old familiar oil and fuel stains on the passenger's side, with footmarks and dirt from some mechanic's feet on the seat.

Shutting the door made me realize that the door locks are much more secure than they used to be, and above my head there was a strong rubber strap which I had to hook over a clip on the door. This is just a safety measure to hold the doors closed should a door lock break. There were two strips of tape right across the top of the windscreen, each strip about 2 in. wide, put there to take the glare out of the sun—should there be any!

Of the row of instruments on the panel the one on the extreme left was an oil temperature gauge for the diff unit oil. This was only fitted because a new type of oil pump was being used for the gearbox and the team were a little apprehensive about it. The gauge was fitted so that the driver could take the odd glance at it to make sure that all was well.

Half facing the driver, on the left of the actual panel, was a speedometer. This was not in use—its readings might have frightened the drivers! The first of the smaller diameter gauges was to record the fuel pressure, then an ammeter, oil temperature gauge, water temperature gauge, rev counter and oil pressure

gauge. The last three I have mentioned could all be seen very clearly through the steering wheel spokes in the dead ahead position.

The leading edge of the facia, which is inclined away from the driver, contains a row of tumbler switches. From left to right they control the side lamps, headlamps, pass lamps, windscreen wipers (single speed wiper which operates at 80 sweeps per minute), an electrically-operated windscreen washer and the dip switch, which is elongated by having a length of rubber tube over the end to bring it closer to the left hand. Then finally there is an over-riding switch which brings the stop lamps into constant operation should the normal tail lamps go on the blink, for it is mandatory to have tail lamps at all times. The only other control on the left side of the column is the horn button, which, although it fulfills the requirements of the rules, in that it blows a horn, makes a noise that would be completely useless on the circuit.

On the right side of the steering column there is another switch which operates in a horizontal plane, and this is for the direction indicators. To the right of that there is the fuel-pump switch and the ignition switch. Within the spread of the hand, about 4in. above these two and slightly to the right, is the starter button. This layout is specifically to help the driver get the car on the move as soon as possible after the Le Mans type start.

Behind, and to the right of the driver's shoulder there is a battery master switch which must have been kicked by somebody leaping into the car, for the Bakelite switch was broken in half. To the right of that again there is a starter motor solenoid so that the driver could still start the engine should the starter button malfunction. On the opposite side of the car, to the left of the passenger seat, is the fuel changeover tap. This used to be a three-way device, but since the two side tanks now have cross-over feed, the tap has but two ways, main and reserve. The reserve tank has only $1\frac{1}{2}$ gallons of fuel, but since this is enough for one lap at Le Mans, it suffices in this case. 4 ☞

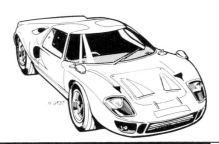

H.6437

AUTOCAR December 12 1968   AUTOCAR December 12 1968

Above: Innes Ireland thunders through the mist on the deserted Silverstone circuit, finding out how the Le Mans winner feels

Left: Of course, things do not always go right . . . the GT40 crawls back onto the tarmac after its excursion into the cabbage patch

Right: Driver's eye view—the headlamp flasher, with the long tube extension, is essential for 208 mph motoring down the Mulsanne Straight

Below right: Travel-stained stern. The lens on the right wing is for the green identification lamp

AUTOCAR December 12 1968

HAPPINESS...
GT 40 LeMANS

5

AUTOCAR December 12 1968

Despite the fog and slippery track, happiness just is driving the Le Mans-winning GT40

"So that's the mill . . ." A pensive look at the 5-litre Ford engine, cylinder heads by Gurney-Weslake and carburettors by Weber

Below left: Cockpit check, and Ireland looks at the fuel tank cocks on the rear bulkhead. The door safety strap can be seen hanging down

List of Suppliers

Lubricating oil	GULF OIL CORPORATION
Tyres	FIRESTONE
Cylinder heads	WESLAKE ENGINEERING LTD.
	COOPERS MECHANICAL JOINTS
Gaskets	ANGLO-AMERICAN RACERS
Main and big end bearings	VANDERVELL PRODUCTS
Transistor ignition, alternator and starter	AUTOLITE DIVISION FORD MOTOR CO.
Spark plugs	AUTOLITE
Carburettors	WEBER
Carburettor ball joints	ROSE FORGROVE
Fuel pumps	STEWART WARNER
Fuel filter	F.I.S.P.A.
Fuel lines	SUPERFLEXIT
Oil filter	FRAM
Oil lines	SIMPLIFIX
	HUBERT TRIST
Alternator belt	GATES
Starter ring gear	F. B. WILMOTT
Rubber bushes	SILENTBLOC
Clutch	BORG and BECK
Transmission	ZAHNRADFABRIK FRIEDRICHSHAFEN
Drive shafts and universal joints	B.R.D.
Drive shaft couplings	METALASTIK
Brakes	GIRLING
Friction material	FERODO
Wheel castings	AEROPLANE and MOTOR CASTINGS
Wheel bearings	BRITISH TIMKEN
Suspension joints	SOUTH WEST PRODUCTS SHAFER
Road springs	TEMPERED SPRING
Exhaust pipes	T.D.C. COMPONENTS
Steering rack	CAM GEARS
Needle roller bearings	I.N.A.
Steering column and gear shift universal joints	BORG-WARNER
Steering wheel	J. A. PEARCE
Battery	EXIDE
Lighting system	CIBIE
	SYLVANIA
Screen wiper	LUCAS
Screen wiper arm and blade	TRICO
Switches	LUCAS
Instruments	SMITHS
	C.A.V.
Radiators	SERCK
Dampers	KONI
Fuel cells	GOODYEAR
Chassis frame	ABBEY PANELS
Body panels	GLASS FIBRE ENGINEERING
Door locks	WILMOT BREEDEN
Paint	IMPERIAL CHEMICAL INDUSTRIES
Exhaust pipe paint	SPEREX
Glass	TRIPLEX
Windscreen fixative	DUNLOP CHEMICAL DIVISION
Rear light fixative	BITUMEN INDUSTRIES
Body fasteners	H. K. PORTER
Seats	WOOD and PICKETT

General Machining and Metal Fabrications

W. A. D. LAWRENCE	A.E.B. PANELS
FLETCHER BROCK and COLLIS	GOMM METAL DEVELOPMENTS
MATHEWS ENGINEERING	GILBERT and RICKARD
WENTWORTH ENGINEERING	BRITISH ERMETO CORPN.
HELDREW ENGINEERING	METAL COLOURS
SOUTH EAST ENGINEERING	ARCH MOTORS
RAPIDE ENGINEERING	A.P.G.

Services

Spray painting	RON WEBB
Exhaust pipe painting	HANKOE MICROBLAST
Balancing	JACK BRABHAM MOTORS
Argonarc welding	SOUTHBOROUGH SHEET METAL LOLA CARS
Inspection and crack detection	HOWSONS INSPECTION SERVICES

The Ford GT40 as I knew it had the performance to win at Le Mans even as far back as 1965. But the limiting factor in those days was the engine, for we could only rev it to 5,500 in the gears and a little over 6,000 rpm in top. John Wyer has found a great deal of reliability and extra performance by using the Gurney-Weslake cylinder heads fitted to the 5-litre Ford V8 engine, and this is perhaps the greatest single factor in making the car a successful one.

Gearbox lubrication is another thing that has come under scrutiny, and a new oil pump has been devised. It is a simple circulatory device and after the oil is pumped through a radiator to cool it, it goes into a gallery along the top of the crown wheel. This has holes drilled in it, and the oil merely drips down on the crownwheel, and supplies lubrication in addition to the splash pick up that was previously the sole means.

The only parts of the car that had been touched since finishing at Le Mans were the big end bearings. For the first time these had been supplied by Vandervell, who had done a great deal of work in conjunction with JW Engineering in this direction. The only reason that they had been changed was that Vandervell wished to have the bearings out of the car to put on display at their stand at the Motor Show.

The modifications in this area were mainly to the con rods where the surface finish of the area that comes in contact with the back of the bearing shell was much improved. This gave a better contact area, which greatly assisted the heat transfer rate from bearing to con rod.

One of the old troubles was oil surge. This has now been eliminated to a great extent by fitting a sump with an improved baffle system and larger oil pump rotors.

As far as the bodywork and style is concerned, there are few changes to the cars I drove in 1965. The wheel arches have been enlarged to accommodate the wider tyres which now have a tread width of 8 in. front and 12½ in. rear. But the most significant improvements are in the construction of the body panels themselves.

To give greater resilience and strength the glass fibre has been reinforced with long fibres of carbon filament which are matted together. In the solid state, this carbon filament is used for aero engine turbine blades and has just recently been taken off the secret list. The material was developed by the Royal Aircraft Establishment at Farnborough, and was talked about recently in Raymond Baxter's BBC TV programme—"Tomorrow's World".

Having assimilated this great store of knowledge of what everything did and how to do it, I finally managed to get the engine started, left the pit area and drove into the fog. After a couple of laps to warm up the gear and axle oil, I started to go a bit faster. It has become painfully obvious that the Le Mans ratios were not at all suited to Silverstone, for I was going round 85 to 90 mph corners in second gear with only about 5,000 rpm on the clock on the exits!

Ron Easton, our photographer and Martin Lewis, the chap who sits across the desk from me, were out at one of the corners, and I was determined to give them a good photograph to take back to the office. This was my first mistake.

I had not allowed myself nearly enough time to get accustomed to the car and realize just how different it was in handling characteristic since I last drove one. I came rushing into the corner after the pits, changed down into second and gave the car a good flick into the corner. Unfortunately, the track was terribly greasy and wet, and it just wouldn't flick. By this time I was scratching about a bit and although the car started to go round the corner, I was about to run out of road on the exit. So I gave the throttle a bit of a jab to bring the tail out—and bring the tail out it did. I don't think I've ever gone sideways for quite so long and finally I could see that I was fighting a losing battle—it just wasn't getting any better. Hoping against hope that Ron Easton had his fog-penetrating lens in action, I jabbed on the brakes and spun the car neatly to a stop—although by this time I was some 10 yards off the road on the infield. My only consolation was in the thought that John Wyer, in letting me drive the car, was probably expecting something of the sort.

Having learnt the lesson that these very wide tyres are not so forgiving I progressed round the circuit. I had to use second gear for several corners and never managed more than 5,700 rpm in fourth gear. But even this was producing 147 mph. The gear change itself was very light, quick and positive, with the exception of coming out of fourth gear, when the lever was very sticky and I had to pull it very hard.

The brakes worked perfectly, and although I couldn't put them on really hard because of the greasy track, they retained that secure, hardish feeling pressure that is such a comfort at the end of the Mulsanne straight when you are doing 208 mph.

One thing in particular has changed dramatically—and that is the steering. It seems to be very sensitive indeed, and I had to be very delicate with the wheel. This is now a very small 13 in. affair and the front wheels were sensitive to the slightest turn. It kicked in my hands quite a bit, and I found it was very easy to overcorrect in the prevailing conditions. This rather put me off having too much of a go with the car—mainly because I knew it was going to the Turin Motor Show the following morning. But then again, I think this condition is aggravated, or enlarged by the very wide tyres which didn't seem to grip at all well in the wet.

But still I had great fun. In spite of the very high gearing, which gives 205 plus at Le Mans, I could feel a tremendous response to the throttle. Bearing in mind that the car was virtually untouched since its mammoth mileage of 2,766.89 during the 24 hours of Le Mans, I was staggered to find that everything functioned so well.

I think this in itself is a great credit to all the team at JW Automotive Engineering who have put such a tremendous amount of hard work into the GT 40 cars over the years. And a great deal of credit must be given to the Gulf Oil Company, for it is really their support of the project and the faith they had in it, that has allowed the team to develop the car to the race-winning form that it has shown this year. Not only has it won races, but the Manufacturers Championship for sports cars as well.

OWNER'S VIEW

Many owners of GT40s have enjoyed brief flirtations with the car, sampling its delights before moving on to new exotica, but Steven Smith, head of Music Hire Group Ltd, has had a long association with the GT40, buying his car in 1970 and using it both for racing and for commuting to and from work.

JSA: Why are you interested in the GT40?

SS: Because I think it is the last of the sports racing cars that can sensibly be driven on the road, and its performance is so highly impressive. Many people don't realise what performance it has, and think the car is a souped-up Marcos or something.

JSA: When did you buy your GT40?

SS: I saw it for sale in 1970, at the London Sports Car Centre, and, as I had always liked the car, decided to buy it. 1969 had been a very busy year for me at work, and I felt that I deserved some relaxation, which the GT40 could provide.

JSA: What sort of condition was the car in at the time?

SS: It had 53,000 miles on the speedo, which is quite high for a GT40, and it did need some attention. The electrical system was poor, with the windscreen wipers not working, some lights out and so on, but that was relatively

easy to cure. Over the first three months that I owned the car there were other problems, such as the suspension, which was very clattery, needing some of the bearings replacing. Although 1013 was a road car, it had seen some racing use, and is reputed to have done 50,000 miles by the time Willie Green drove it in the Vila Real 6-hour race.

JSA: Have you had to do much in the way of renovation since then?

SS: Oh yes! The car is currently undergoing its second rebuild following a rust cure. Corrosion is a problem, but apart from that the car has been relatively trouble free. The first time it received a rust cure I replaced the bottom half to three quarters of an inch of the chassis tub. I had made the mistake of running the car through the first winter I owned it, and that had caused it to deteriorate.

JSA: Did you use it when there was snow and ice on the roads?

SS: Yes, and you probably can't imagine what it's like to drive a GT40 in such conditions, especially when the car has rear tyres that are twelve inches wide: it could not cope with even gentle gradients in snow. It may seem like heresy, to have used the car like that, but at the time GT40s were not the vauable cars they are now.

JSA: How extensive is the second rebuild?

SS: This time the lower eight inches of the chassis have had to be replaced. Bryan Wingfield has completed that part of the operation, but I still have to re-assemble the car. Unfortunately, I don't expect to finish until Autumn 1983.

JSA: Have you needed to replace any other major components?

SS: I fitted alloy fuel tanks, of course, as the bag tanks had started to leak, as they all do. The engine is the one which was in the car when I bought it. It had been rebuilt shortly before I acquired the car, but suffered misfiring problems and broke some piston rings. I had it rebored, and fitted new rings,

shortly before taking the car to Le Mans in 1973 for the fiftieth anniversary parades.

JSA: How reliable has the transmission been?

SS: There have been no gearbox problems, and the clutch has never seized on my car, even though I no longer use it during winter; in fact, the car has been in bits for the last two winters. I always ensure that there is inhibiting oil in the bores when I put the car aside for the winter.

JSA: Have you experienced any problems in locating spare parts?

SS: Not in the long run, but you cannot expect to get hold of parts immediately. It helps, of course, to know where to go, but most parts are available in the end. Some time ago the petrol pump expired, and until I could get a replacement Stewart-Warner unit I had to use an SU as a temporary measure; it was cobbled together with assorted bits of flexible pipe, clips and so on, but it worked until I could get the correct unit. Many of the parts used in the car are obtainable easily, if you know what other cars are fitted with them. The spark plugs, for example, are the same as those fitted to certain Cortinas. Engine spares generally are easy to obtain, and such items as gaskets and oil filters can be obtained from Ford agents dealing with American Fords. Some of the spares can be very expensive – the catches which hold down the front and rear body sections are the same as those on Vickers Viscount engines, and cost around £70 each! Now you know why more and more GT40s are having different fasteners fitted!

JSA: I believe there are other aircraft parts fitted to GT40s; the wiper motors, on Mark IIs at least, are from Boeing 707 designs.

SS: That is very likely, as some needle roller bearings in the suspension are as used in the flaps of 707s.

JSA: What sort of performance and handling does your car have?

SS: Performance, shattering; roadholding, good. I have never timed the car's acceleration, but I know it is very, very quick.

JSA: I recall some years ago when you had the car at Croft, you gave me a demonstration of its performance on the race track there, and sitting in the passenger seat I was quite astonished by its roadholding; I simply couldn't believe that any car could go through the chicane that fast.

SS: But I wasn't driving in a serious fashion! If you had been in Maggie Blankstone's GT40 at Croft you would know just how quickly a GT40 could be driven! I used to race the GT40 in a very gentlemanly fashion, not seriously at all. Setting up a GT40 to get the best out of it requires an awful lot of patience too. There is no castor adjustment on the front wheels, and toe in is easy at the front. The rear suspension is a very different matter. The rear castor angle is difficult to measure, as there is nothing to gauge it with. It is also possible to end up with the car going crabwise, if the rear wheels are not correctly aligned.

JSA: How practical is your car for road use, and are the running costs high?

SS: It's hopelessly impractical! For example, you need a lot of room when parking, or you won't be able to get out of it. The doors include part of the roof section, so, unless they can be opened fully, you would have to crawl out. There is no room inside the car for any luggage, as mine doesn't have the two luggage boxes which are fitted to some GT40s. However, there is a little space in the spare wheel compartment, as I do not carry a spare in my car; instead I rely on a couple of aerosol inflators if I get a puncture. The engine is fairly tractable, but very heavy on fuel; around town consumption can be as bad as 10mpg, and the best I ever got was 18 miles per gallon when cruising at a steady 70mph on a motorway. Fortunately the carburation needs little attention, and I prefer to leave mine alone if possible, adjusting the slow-running jets only when absolutely necessary.

JSA: Do you intend to use the GT40 in motorsport when you get it back together?

SS: Yes, but most likely only for hillclimbing. I am involved with the Harewood Hillclimb, and am looking forward to competing there again with the GT40.

JSA: Have you found the Owners Club useful to you?

SS: Very much so, as Bryan Wingfield, the Club Secretary, has been very helpful, and he undertook the car's recent chassis rebuild. The Club is no longer active on the social side, but I consider Bryan to be a very worthwhile GT40 specialist, and I can always call on him for advice.

JSA: Have you found any other specialists to be particularly helpful?

SS: It is surprising how much help can be obtained from the competitions departments of parts suppliers. When I had some clutch trouble shortly before a race, I contacted Automotive Products, who overhauled the offending parts that same day! Competition departments are geared up for rapid response, and should not be overlooked if your GT40 needs urgent repairs.

JSA: What advice would you give to potential owners of the GT40?

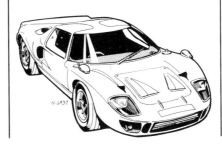

SS: Don't buy one! GT40s are very expensive to maintain, and unless you either own a garage or are very rich, the GT40 would be a real problem. It helps if you are a do-it-yourself type, as otherwise garage bills will be enormous. There is a saying about boats, that an owner can expect annual costs to be about 10% of the boat's value; I think the same holds true for the GT40. Insurance is, of course, extremely expensive, with £700 per annum being typical. A GT40 should ideally be kept warm and dry during winter, so consider also the costs of providing a heated garage. All in all, a GT40 can be a very costly car, but a marvellous experience!

Super Profile

BUYING

"Ford GT40. 4.7 engine ZF box. New tyres. Spare set of wheels with wet tyres. U.K. duty paid. Immaculate. £3,500 ono. Serious enquiries only to ...."

Advertisements such as this, which appeared in 1971 in the British magazine *Motoring News,* were quite common during the early seventies. GT40s have never been cheap, but they were fairly affordable exotica which started life at around £7000 in 1965 and steadily depreciated to some £3,500 in 1971. From then they showed a gradual increase in price which began to accelerate rapidly until, in 1974, the going rate was £10,000 or thereabouts. Subsequent increases in value have been spectacular, so that any quoted price is outdated by the time it appears in print. The result is that very few can afford to buy a GT40, but those who do are assured of a fast-appreciating asset which provides a splendid hedge against inflation.

Nowadays GT40s tend to change hands without being advertised, and any potential buyer may have to search hard to find one. Perhaps the most likely places to look for advertisements for GT40s are the pages of *Motor Sport* in Britain, *Road & Track* and *Autoweek* in the USA, but a better

solution would be to contact the Owners' Club, who could easily put the buyer in touch with current owners.

GT40 prices are so high that any potential owner is unlikely to be too concerned if the car he intends purchasing requires remedial work to some degree, for the chances are that he will be able to afford it without losing much sleep. There are, however, certain aspects of the GT40 which deserve serious consideration, as they could significantly affect the price involved in any deal. Easily the most serious problem which afflicts the GT40 is RUST, for the steel monocoques received little or no anti-corrosion treatment when new, and many of these cars now suffer badly from the ravages of time and salt encrusted roads. They rot particularly badly in the sills, and once rust has a firm hold there is little alternative to having a full chassis rebuild: a major operation which will be both costly and time consuming. As original chassis are no longer available for spares, and chassis jigs have long since vanished, the job of rebuilding a rusted chassis is not easy, and will inevitably be expensive.

Another area of the car which deteriorates rapidly with age is the fuel tanks, and it is wise to replace these during any chassis rebuild. The original bag tanks tend to perish, resulting in leakage of fuel into the sills. There are no longer any stocks of bag tanks, posing a problem for those who wish to keep their cars authentic, but most owners are happy to replace them with alloy tanks, which are much more durable and can be installed relatively easily.

Mechanical problems in the GT40 are comparatively rare, as might be expected from a car robust enough to put up with 24 hours of hard driving at Le Mans. The Ford V8, in both its 289 and 302 versions, is as strong as an ox, and in normal use can be expected to last for 100,000 miles with thorough routine maintenance. If

the purchaser is unfortunate enough to acquire a GT40 whose engine has seen better days, there is still no need to worry, for complete engines are commonplace (they went into large numbers of Mustangs, Cobras, Galaxies and the like) and can be obtained at prices which are trivial in comparison with the value of the car. Engine specifications vary considerably, ranging from mild single-carburetted 230bhp 289s up to Gurney-Weslake-headed 302s, which can be rated at anything up to 465bhp when fitted with four Webers. Even with the lowest output engine, performance is terrific, for with only about one ton to propel, the power/weight ratio is excellent and compares favourably with virtually all supercars. The potential owner may be tempted to opt for a full-race engine, but whilst it might be very satisfying to know that one's car is capable of 200mph, for all practical purposes such an engine would be too temperamental, and could result in a car that is both difficult and embarrassing to drive.

The GT40's transmission is appropriately sturdy, the ZF gearbox being strong and pleasant to use. If it should require attention, then a specialist is called for, as it is extremely complicated and very difficult to work on. During their racing days JW Automotive and Ford Advanced Vehicles employed fitters who worked solely on the gearboxes; when attending races the team took with them spare gearboxes with differing ratios, so that the entire gearbox could be changed as necessary without having to resort to working on the gearbox internals. One transmission problem which seems to afflict a great many GT40s concerns the clutch; although it is adequately strong, and does not suffer unduly from wear, it does have a tendency to seize when not used regularly. Lack of use causes more problems than does excess use, and so many GT40s are put aside over winter each year that spring sees a rash of

28

seized clutches being discovered.

There can be few owners of collectible cars who take adequate precautions when laying up their cars for the winter, so a potential owner would be well advised to check a car thoroughly to ensure that such items as oil seals and wheel bearings have not suffered from neglect.

In recent years much emphasis has been placed on the authenticity of individual cars, and it is worth taking the trouble to discover a GT40's history before parting with a significant sum of money to acquire it. It has happened on more than one occasion that a crashed vehicle has been rebuilt into two cars. First a new chassis has been used with original mechanical parts then, at a later date, someone has obtained the written-off chassis, straightened it, and built a new car upon it. It is difficult to say which car is authentic, and opinions will no doubt differ, but it is as well to be aware of the facts before coming to your own conclusion.

Which model?

GT40s and their derivatives fall into four main categories: small block cars in three versions, Road, Race and "civilised" Mark III, and the big-block Mark IIs. The initially very thin dividing line between road and race specification has become more blurred as time has passed, and the two types are generally no longer distinguishable from each other. Basically, a former racing car will always be worth more than a road car, all other things being equal, on the grounds that its history is so much more fascinating: "never raced or rallied" is not a good selling point where GT40s are concerned. The Mark III ought, by rights, to be the most desirable of all, as it combines limited production with a level of convenience and practicality which

is unmatched by any other model, but its non-racing pedigree counts against it, and its styling is arguably less attractive than that of its more businesslike brethren.

The two models to aim for are the Gulf GT40s, which took the marque to its pinnacle of development, and the Mark II, which, with its massive 427inch engine, epitomises for many the true American sports car, and gave the type its first Le Mans victory. The problems associated with Mark IIs are much the same as for the smaller-engined cars, although an owner has the added worry of the custom-built T-44 gearbox, which is no longer available. Happily the gearbox's internals are Ford Galaxie-based, so spares can probably be improvised; if all else fails a Hewland gearbox ought to be able to accept the engine's enormous torque, but will be less easy to use.

The Mark V

Early in 1981 a new GT40 entered the marketplace; with the authority of both Ford and J W Automotive Engineering, who own the production rights to the car, Safir Engineering commenced the production of a limited series of brand new GT40s, to be known as the Mark V. The Mark V resulted from Safir's founder, Peter Thorp, being unable to find a GT40 at the right price and in the right condition to suit him. He employed Len Bailey to redesign the monocoque to enable it to be produced more

easily, with folded panels replacing the original pressings. Bailey took the opportunity to incorporate into the car certain other design modifications that he had had in mind, the result being a car which incorporates few parts in common with the original, but is still very much a GT40. The Mark V may also benefit owners of earlier versions, as certain sub-assemblies, such as the front suspension, will fit on older cars, for which the original parts stock has long since run out.

The principal problem associated with the Mark V is that of getting it registered for road use, as it has difficulty in complying with legislation in many countries. Despite that, three cars, commencing with number GT40P/1090, had been built by June 1982. There are those who consider the Mark V to be a replica, rather than the real thing, but examination of the car will convince most people that it is a very real GT40. The car incorporates all the essential ingredients of a true GT40, at a price which is only about two-thirds that of an earlier model.

CLUBS, SPECIALISTS & BOOKS

Owning a GT40 can be a marvellous experience which rapidly turns sour when mechanical problems baffle those who have never before worked on such a car, and when location of the correct spare parts seems to be impossible. It is for such occasions that membership of the appropriate club is an absolute necessity, for often it is only through the knowledge accumulated within a club that such problems can be solved. With some 32 GT40s currently resident in the UK, and about 48 in the USA, it is hardly surprising that these two countries are the only ones to boast GT40 clubs.

Clubs

The GT40 Owners Club in the UK is run by Bryan Wingfield, of South Gibcracks Farm, Bicknacre Road, East Hanningfield, Chelmsford, Essex CM3 5MP. As well as offering help and advice to members, Bryan is well qualified to work on GT40s, having rebuilt the crashed GT40P/1009 to concours condition some years ago. The club is able to replace any chassis which is rusted or damaged beyond repair, as much tooling has now been manufactured. However, it must be pointed out that such chassis are available only to *bona fide* owners, and new cars will *not* be made. Many other parts are available via the club, a recent addition to stocks being previously unobtainable windscreens.

In the USA there is no club catering solely for GT40 owners, but their interests are taken care of by the **Shelby American Automobile Club,** who can be contacted via their Director, Richard J Kopec, of 22 Olmstead Road, West Redding, CT 06896. The club believes that ''ownership isn't important ...enthusiasm is'', and produces an excellent 64-page glossy magazine five times a year to keep members in touch.

Specialists

Many of the specialists who now work on GT40s were with the teams who raced those cars in their heyday. **J R Etheridge Ltd,** 125 High Road, Bushey Heath, Watford, Herts WD2 1JA, England, not only has its proprietor, John Etheridge, as an ex-Ford Advanced Vehicles man, but enjoys the services of Ford Advanced Vehicles' electrician, Bill Pink. The company is principally concerned with Bristol, Ferrari and Aston Martin (there are not many GT40s around!) but is able to provide full facilities for GT40s. Another company using former FAV personnel is **Oldham & Crowther,** 27-31 Ivatt Way, Westwood industrial Estate, Peterborough PE3 7PH, England. They too have to service other makes (Jaguar in this case), but are happy to cope with GT40s, Lolas and other exotica. **Safir Engineering Limited,** Brooklands Industrial Park, Weybridge, Surrey, England, have as their main line of business the production of heavily modified Land-Rovers and Range-Rovers, even producing some with six-wheel drive. Their MkV GT40 is intended in part to display their engineering skills, but its production has resulted in the better availability of spares which will fit, or can be adapted for, earlier models. Peter Thorp and Jim Rose (who worked for Alan Mann Racing in its GT40 days) are the people to contact there. GT40 motive power in the UK is often provided by **Mathwall Engineering,** of Thursley, Surrey, England, who have long specialised in the preparation of Ford V8s. The remains of J W Automotive's original parts inventory are now held by Hofmann & Mountfort Ltd., Fairfield Works, Reading Road, Henley-on-Thames, Oxon, England.

In the USA there has never been any problem in finding firms specialising on Ford V8s, but the tremendous size of the country makes it difficult for anyone to become established as a specialist on such a marque as the GT40. **McCluskey Ltd,** of 23890 Madison Street, Torrance, CA 90505, USA, provide services for GT40s, as do **Le Mans Garage Inc,** 496 Old Post Road No. 3, Greenwich, CT 06830, USA. Carburation problems can be dealt with by **Inglese Weber Induction Systems** of 186 N. Main Street, Branford, CT 06405, USA.

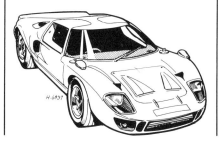

H.6937

Books

There have been several books dealing with the GT40, but regrettably most of them are no longer in print, although copies may perhaps still be found in specialist motoring bookshops.

Ford: The Dust and the Glory (Leo Levine 1968/ Macmillan) covers the cars' racing history in depth, with emphasis on the American involvement.

The Inside Story of the Fastest Fords (Karl E Ludvigsen 1970/ Style Auto) is a well illustrated history of the cars' design and development.

The Certain Sound (John Wyer 1981/ Edita) deals with the story from the British viewpoint, with much fascinating detail of the finances and politics involved in setting up and running a racing organisation.

The Racing Fords (Hans Tanner 1968/ Meredith) deals with the cars' history up to Le Mans 1967; well illustrated, although including some text from the SAE papers.

The Ford GT40 Prototypes and Sports Cars (David Hodges 1970/ Leventhal) is a small book containing a useful chassis number checklist and an extensive racing record.

Ford versus Ferrari (Anthony Pritchard 1968/ Pelham) looks at the two main protagonists in the 1964 to 1967 sports car racing seasons.

Sports Car Championship (Anthony Pritchard 1972/ Hale) deals with the Ford against Porsche conflicts of 1968 and 1969.

Racing Mechanic (Jeremy Walton 1980/ Osprey) follows the fortunes of FAV and JW mechanic Ermanno Cuoghi through his days with Ford, Porsche and Ferrari.

Ford GT40 SAE Papers (Roy Lunn and others 1966 & 1979/ Motorbooks) is a remarkably detailed look at the technical aspects of sports car design, with the development of the Mark II coming under close scrutiny.

Ford GT40 1964–1978 (R M Clarke 1981/ Brooklands) Reprints of contemporary reports on the GT40, taken from magazines in the UK, USA and Canada.

The Ford GT (William S Stone 1967/ Profile) was first on the market, being a slim paperback with good photographs and artwork.

Video & Records

The popularity of the video recorder has added another dimension to the storage and retrieval of reference material, several race reports now being available on this medium.

La Ronde Infernale (Castrol) The epic struggle for Le Mans 1969, with Ickx (GT40) racing Herrmann's Porsche 908 to the line in the closest finish ever.

This Time Tomorrow (Shell) Le Mans 1966, and Ford's first win with the GT40.

Un Homme et une Femme (Claude Lelouche) Widely regarded as a classic love story, the hero just happens to be a test driver for Ford France; the sight and sound of his GT40 being tested on the banked track at Montlhery is unforgettable.

Mark II GT40s figure strongly on a Decca record, **Le Mans '66,** featuring the sounds of the cars and commentary from Bruce McLaren, Graham Hill, Chris Amon and Carroll Shelby.

PHOTO GALLERY

1. The Lola Mk6 GT had considerable influence on the Ford GT, and the similarity between the two can be seen in this view of the single Lola which escaped the Ford net, going instead to Texas oil millionaire John Mecom Jnr, who fitted it with a Chevrolet engine. The Lola and the Ford shared a common design heritage, but little else; the two had few interchangeable parts.

2. The smooth nose design which was used on the first two prototypes (this is GT/102 at Le Mans) caused excessive lift and admitted insufficient air to the radiator, necessitating three holes to be cut out at the front to improve cooling.

3

4

3. GT/101 (foreground) and GT/102 at the Le Mans Test Days in 1964. The tail sections were without the distinctive spoiler that was found necessary to keep the car on the ground.

4. GT/102 was the first Ford GT actually to start a race, at the Nurburgring in 1964. The nose has received a wide slot to direct air to the radiator, and the long-range lamps have been moved up from the air dam to a position immediately below the headlights. The car retired due to suspension components tearing from the chassis – which received considerable strengthening before its next race appearance.

5

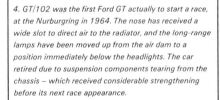

5. Le Mans 1964 saw a three-car team of Fords entered, GT/102 being numbered 10 and entrusted to Phil Hill and Bruce McLaren. The row of vents on the roof was applicable only to the prototypes and to production cars 1000 to 1007. The vents in the rear deck were later re-sited further back. Note the light used to illuminate the racing number for events involving night driving.

6. The FAV team used to stay at the Hotel de France, La Chartre, when racing at Le Mans, and the sight of racing cars in the street outside was not unusual. This is GT/103 (the number is chalked on the front tyre), driven by Richie Ginther and Masten Gregory. Like 102, it retired with a broken gearbox.

6

7. The brunt of the 1965 racing programme was carried out by Shelby American, who used a pair of early prototypes. The frontal treatment was changed by FAV before Shelby received the cars, but Shelby's own modifications included Halibrand alloy wheels, an oil filler pipe extended to a hatch in the rear offside body, and oil-coolers placed alongside the transmission; air for these coolers was taken in via the scoops added to the engine air intakes. This car is GT/103, the Daytona winner, seen at the 1965 Le Mans test weekend. GT/104 was also present, and was used to test an elongated nose section.

8. Continuing development of the car was still in the hands of FAV, who used GT/105 as a test vehicle. Here it sports a slightly higher than usual rear spoiler: the front air dam has a cover taped in place.

9. The test weekends at Le Mans were of immense value in obtaining test data well in advance of the race. GT/105, wearing Dunlop tyres on its Borrani wheels, poses with a Goodyear-shod Borrani and a Firestone-shod Halibrand.

10

11

10 & 11. Since Ferrari's prototypes were generally open cars, and since the configuration seemed to promise less weight, FAV built four open GTs to test the idea out. The cockpit was airier than the closed coupe, but suffered from draughts, and the aerodynamics were less effective. FAV development driver Sir John Whitmore tested GT/111 at Le Mans; his helmet carries the Ford oval reversed, which must have caused problems for printers and photographers alike!

12

13

12, 13 & 14. The arrival of the 7-litre Mark II at Le Mans in 1965 caused quite a stir, the 465bhp monsters being easily the fastest cars that the circuit had ever seen. A lengthened nose, as tried in the test days, was used, and the cars received rear fins and spoilers before the race. This car was GT/106, its brand new sister car being GT/107.

Bruce McLaren and Ken Miles drove car No.1, which retired with gearbox trouble, whilst Phil Hill and Chris Amon were in charge of No.2 which, after setting the best qualifying time of 3 min 33 sec, also succumbed to transmission problems.

14

15

18

16

19

17

20

15. Three brand-new production GT40s appeared at Le Mans in 1965, and all of them were either works or quasi-works entries. 1005 was nominally a Scuderia Filipinetti entry (actually in the charge of Shelby American): it retired with head gasket trouble, but Filipinetti were sufficiently impressed to order two such cars for the 1966 season.

16 & 17. Wearing the blue and white livery of Rob Walker, 1004 took the place of the Serenissima which Walker had entered, but had not been able to obtain. Like the Filipinetti car, 1004 was looked after by Shelby. Driven by Umberto Maglioli and Bob Bondurant, it retired with a blown head gasket.

18, 19 & 20. The third new GT40 was 1006, entered by FAV. It featured the new front-end style known initially as the "Le Mans nose" which, with minor variations, was incorporated on all subsequent GT40s. Not surprisingly, head gasket trouble sidelined this car, which was driven by Innes Ireland and Sir John Whitmore. The engines simply were unable to withstand the stresses imposed on them by the flat-out drive down the Mulsanne Straight.

21

22

24

23

21 & 22. Alan Mann Racing developed a lightweight GT40, incorporating panels in elektron light alloy. The sill panels were removed in the cause of lightness, and the doors and other body panels narrowed slightly so as not to overhang the chassis, while at the rear the side scoops were riveted in place rather than formed into the bodywork. Mark II-style brake cooling scoops were added to the top of the rear deck. Elektron also replaced steel in the construction of the roof. The cars took part in the Sebring 12-hour race and the 1966 Le Mans Test Days where AMGT/1 wore race number "16", and AMGT/2 number "15".

23. Paul Hawkins bought AMGT/2 and campaigned it enthusiastically in 1967 and 1968. The light alloy panels were replaced by fibreglass so as to restore the car to production standards and allow it to compete in the, then, Group 4. It was easily the most successful private entry GT40, helped by its Hewland gearbox which allowed quick changes of ratios ensuring that the car was correctly geared for each circuit visited. Very wide wheels were used, resulting eventually in the front spare-wheel cover having to bulge outwards.

24. Alan Mann also acted as agent for Ford, and several GT40s passed through his hands. Here an unpainted 1019 is shown being tested by Graham Hill at Goodwood in 1965, prior to its being stripped and sent to Holman & Moody.

25

26

27

28

25. Dan Gurney and Jerry Grant very nearly scored the Mark II's first Sebring win in 1966, at the wheel of this blue-painted coupe. On the last lap the car expired when a rod bolt failed: Gurney pushed the car across the finish line. For so doing he was promptly disqualified, as the rules forbade such action. Victory went instead to the red X-1 roadster of Miles and Ruby. Safety standards at Sebring in those days were somewhat different from today's (note the fire hydrant hiding behind a single straw bale).

26. At the Le Mans Test Days in 1966 two Mark IIs were present. Trying too hard on the wet track, Walt Hansgen lost control of his car, on the approach to the Dunlop Bridge, and took to the escape road. The car was demolished, and sadly Hansgen sustained injuries from which he later died. Astonishingly, this car (1011) now awaits a planned rebuild in the USA.

27 & 28. The surviving Mark II from Le Mans was loaned to Alan Mann Racing, and used at Spa in 1966, where it finished second in the 1000km race to a Ferrari 330P3. The Mark II's drivers were Whitmore and Gardner, who were hampered by 1012's appetite for tyres.

29

30

31

32

29, 30, 31 & 32. The Spa 1000km race attracted a strong entry of private GT40s, including a two-car team from Essex Wire, managed by David Yorke, who later was to play an important part in the Gulf-JW racing effort. The Scott/Revson GT40, No.42 (probably 1038), came home third behind the Mark II; the other car (1026) retired. The GT40 used as many proprietary parts as possible: through the windscreen of Jochen Neerpasch's car can be seen the demister outlet – a standard part from a Ford Zephyr!

33

33. Fourth place at Spa was taken by Peter Sutcliffe and Brian Redman, driving the former's green-painted 1009 carrying a Johannesburg registration.

34. The Scuderia Filipinetti had been sufficiently impressed with the GT40 which they had been "loaned" in 1965 to buy a pair for the 1966 season. It appears, however, that only one car, 1039, was actually used that year. It is seen here at Spa where, with Mairesse and Muller driving, it retired. Their second car, 1040, was burnt out during practice for what would have been its first race, at Monza in 1967; subsequently Filipinetti shared a Brescia Corse Car.

35. F English Ltd fielded their new GT40, 1017, for the first time at Spa. It finished in fifth position in the hands of Chris Amon and Innes Ireland.

36. To F English had gone the first customer GT40, 1002, later nicknamed "Felix". It is shown here, in 1965, on one of its early outings driven by David Hobbs.

34

35

36

37 to 40. The Mark II's finest hour was at Le Mans in 1966, where three of the eight cars entered survived to take the first three places at the end of the 24 hours. In a controversial deadheat, victory went to 1046, of Amon and McLaren (photo 37) ahead of the Miles/Hulme car (1015) shown in photo 38 which many regard as the moral victor, it having led for most of the latter part of the race, Miles slowed to let the other car catch up, but was relegated to second position when it

was announced that the McLaren/Amon car, having started further back on the grid, had covered a greater distance in the 24 hours and was therefore the winner.

At the back of the Andretti/Bianchi Mark II (1031), photo 39, can be seen the two luggage boxes which the rules required be carried!

Photo 40 shows the Hawkins/Donohue Mark II (1016), which was in trouble on the first lap when a driveshaft failed.

41 & 42. Comparison of the front of a Mark II (the Gurney/Grant Le Mans car, 1047) with the Ford France GT40 of Guy Ligier and Bob Grossman, shows the Mark II's deeper front fenders. fully vented spare wheel cover and quick-lift jacking points.

43

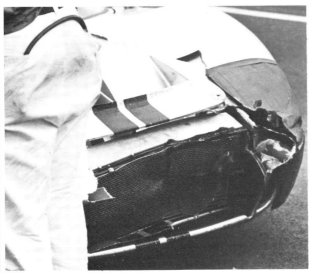

44

45

43, 44 & 45. Scuderia Bear's rarely illustrated GT40, 1029, was at the centre of an incident which nearly caused the withdrawal of the entire Ford works contingent from Le Mans in 1966. During practice the car was being driven rather slowly in the White House area when Dick Thompson's much faster-driven Mark II came across it suddenly and savaged it from behind. The Mark II suffered only superficial damage, but the GT40 left the track and was wrecked. Both Thompson and, oddly, his car were disqualified for "unsportsmanlike conduct" in failing to stop at the scene of the accident and failing to report it to marshals on his return to the pits! Ford, via Leo Beebe, responded that if the officials were unaware of the accident then the circuit must be considered dangerous, and Ford would have to withdraw all their cars. Faced with the possibility of the race becoming a non-event, the organisers relented and re-instated the car, although Thompson's disqualification was allowed to stand. Co-driver Graham Hill, seen here at the wheel, shared the car (XGT2) with Thompson's replacement, Brian Muir.

46

47

48

49

46. A project to build the ultimate lightweight GT40 was begun in 1966, with backing from Ford of Britain. The first prototype was almost complete when word of the programme reached the top brass at Dearborn, who were not amused by this potential rival to the Mark II. Work on the new car promptly stopped, and it was disassembled (the suspension found its way to Essex Wire), the chassis being hidden away until the political climate became more favourable. The sale of Ford Advanced vehicles to John Wyer enabled the car to be resurrected, the chassis being retrieved and built up into the first Mirage – shown here on its first public outing at the Le Mans Test Weekend in 1967.

47 & 48. Comparison of Mirage 1002 with a Ford France GT40 shows clearly the Mirage's slimmer roofline and sleeker sides, with scoops replaced by NACA ducts. Both cars are seen testing variations of nose ducting: the full-flow type had been homologated on the GT40 in time for the 1967 Sebring race.

49. 1967 saw also the arrival of the Mark IIB. The most noticeable difference between it and the earlier model, retrospectively called Mark IIA, was the deletion of the air ducting leading to the front brakes. This particular car was raced at Le Mans by Shelby American, before being loaned to Ford France who ran it at Rheims (where it won) and at Mugello and Montlhery, both times finishing fourth.

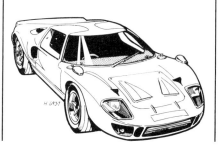

50

51

52

53

50, 51, 52 & 53. The late sixties saw GT40s becoming
increasingly popular with private entrants, who often
modified the cars to keep them competitive. Photo 50
shows Peter Sutcliffe's second GT40, GT/112, which he
had rebuilt from a roadster. Note the BRM alloy wheels
which became standard wear on racing GT40s. Seen at
the same event, at Brands Hatch in 1967, is Eddie
Nelson's GT40, 1009, in photo 51. This car was ex-
Sutcliffe.

Terry Drury owned a variety of GT40s, including
1073, seen at the Nurburgring 1000kms in 1968 in
photo 52. The car displays extensions to the rear spoiler
and some front canard fins, although GT40s usually
managed well enough without such appendages. 1002
went a stage further, being fitted with a perspex wing
for the BOAC 500 mile race in 1968 (photo 53).
Entered by David Prophet Racing, the car had its sill
panels removed, and the two stiffening ribs pressed into
the chassis are clearly visible.

55

56

54 & 55. The combination of Jacky Ickx, GT40, rain and Spa-Francorchamps could be guaranteed to produce a spectacular drive: after winning there in a Mirage in 1967, Ickx took GT40 1075 to victory in 1968. His co-driver in the GT40 was Brian Redman, who drove brilliantly but was still 10 seconds per lap slower, such was Ickx's pace. Gulf GT40s were always immaculately turned out, and were models of careful preparation. The team's approach was intensely professional, and John Wyer, David Yorke and company were so successful that Porsche eventually retained their services en bloc for the 1970 and 1971 seasons. 1075 is probably the most successful racing car of all time, with six wins in major events, including two at Le Mans, and some 11,960 racing miles to its credit.

56. The slippery track at Spa was the undoing of several cars – including three GT40s: the Mairesse/Beurlys car, 1079, seen here as it rounds La Source, slid off the road at Blanchimont.

57

57. While their regular car, 1074, was being overhauled, Hawkins and Hobbs were entrusted with 1004 for Spa. The car had not raced since Le Mans 1965, after which it had been used as a Shelby display car. Dismantled and stored at Slough for some years, it was brought up to Gulf standards (albeit slightly heavier than the others) and used by JW for the one race. Only the old-style door handles differentiate it from the other Gulf cars. It was renumbered 1084 prior to being sold.

58. Who would deny that the GT40 is a work of art? In 1970 an example of Ford's automotive sculpture displayed its classic lines at that most prestigious centre of the Arts, the Louvre in Paris.

58

59

60

59. This unidentified GT40, wearing BRM wheels and still unadorned with stripes and racing roundels, appears to be a standard racing version as it lacks the Ford badges and letters, on sill and nose, which typified road cars.

60 & 61. 1053 was painted Swan White when despatched to its first owner, Vic Damone, in the USA on 31st October 1966. It spent most of its early years in California and was therefore able to avoid the rust which has afflicted so many cars. It is seen here in the yellow and black livery it received after returning to the UK. (Photos: Antoine Chavan, Lausanne).

61

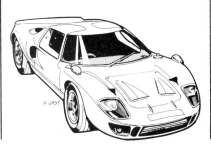

62

63

64

65

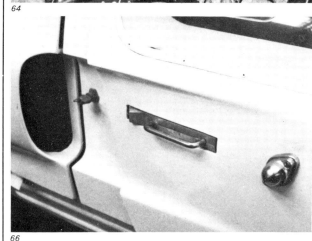

66

67

62. One of the first prototypes under construction. The rubber ''doughnut'' Metalastic joints can clearly be seen, as can the air vents in the side of the bulkhead. Steelwork on early chassis was painted dark blue.

63. On a racing car, accessibility is of paramount importance if valuable seconds are not to be lost during pit-stops. The front of the engine is reached through a large hatch in the rear bulkhead as can be seen here on 1078. The proximity of the engine, including the four hungry Webers, to the interior of the car helps explain the considerable noise level to be endured in the cockpit.

64. Air horns are evidence that 1006 had been used on the road prior to arriving at John Etheridge's London premises for restoration.

65. The underside of a GT40's chassis is rarely seen. Here is 1081, whilst being restored by present owner Henri Bercher.

66. The original door handles were beautifully streamlined, but difficult to grab in the haste of a Le Mans start; several cars, including 1020 here, used a rather unsophisticated addition to facilitate entry. The small light affixed to the door provided illumination of the competition number during night racing.

67. Chassis numbers can be found on a plate on the rear bulkhead, either alongside the radiator header tank or in a similar position inside the cockpit. (Photos 63-67, Henri Bercher, Mont-sur-Rolle).

C1

C2

C1. For Le Mans in 1968 the usual two-car team of Gulf GT40s was strengthened by the addition of a third car, 1076 (foreground), to be driven by Brian Muir and Jack Oliver. Unfortunately, Muir rammed it into the sand at Mulsanne during the first hour, and wrecked the clutch whilst trying to extricate it. 1074 (centre), was shared by Paul Hawkins and David Hobbs; it retired with a blown engine, cause unknown, having previously undergone a clutch change. The sole survivor of the trio was 1075, which had an uneventful race, being driven to a well deserved victory by Pedro Rodriguez and Lucien Bianchi. On most circuits the 1968 Gulf GT40 was as fast as had been the 7-litre Mark IIs of the previous year, showing the merits of the smaller engined car's lighter construction.

C2. For shooting the Steve McQueen film Le Mans, Solar Productions sought a car which could accommodate both a driver and a cameraman with equipment, and which could provide a stable camera platform while running at high speed in company with Porsche 917s and Ferrari 512Ss. Not unnaturally they chose a GT40, the type having already proven its worth in the filming of Grand Prix. The car selected was 1074, which started life as Mirage M1/10003 before being rebuilt as a Gulf GT40 for the 1968 season. It was turned into a roadster and sold to Solar for filming in 1970; when shooting was complete it was offered for sale for the princely sum of £3,150! The car has since been rebuilt as a standard GT40, and now resides in the USA.

C3

C3,C4,C5 & C6. On November 28, 1966, GT40P/1063, resplendent in metallic bronze paintwork, left Slough on its way to the USA. After several years of neglect it was acquired by its present owner, Gary W Kohs, of the Marketing Corporation of America, Birmingham, Michigan. A two and a half year rebuild was completed in June 1982 and the car may now be described as, quite simply, flawless.

C4

C5

C6

C7

C8

C9

C7,C8 & C9. This superbly turned out GT40 is 1059, a road car which is part of the collection of classic cars owned by Jack Frost, M.D., of St Donatus, Iowa. Although it has covered only 2,500 miles, the car has been fully restored by the owner and his six sons. The only mechanical modifications relate to attempts to eliminate totally the possibility of engine compartment fires; steel braided fuel hose has been used, and an onboard fire extinguishing system is fitted to both engine bay and passenger compartment. (Photos by Michael M Frost, St Donatus, Iowa).

C10

C11

C10 & C11. Essex Wire owned three GT40s, their first being 1010, which was extensively damaged at Oulton Park in 1966. The remains were acquired by Peter Sadler, who rebuilt the car and used it with considerable success in international events in 1968 and 1969. Later converted for road use, 1010 eventually passed to its present owner, Brian Poole, of Daventry, Northants, who has restored it to concours condition. The spare wheel cover is of the style usually associated with the Mark III.

C12. The Scuderia Filipinetti had less than the best of luck with its racing cars. They had a GT40 crash at Le Mans in 1966, lost a Dino 206S to fire at the Nurburgring in 1967, and wrecked a Corvette 427 at Le Mans in 1968. This GT40, 1040, was almost destroyed when it caught fire at Monza in 1967, but Filipinetti retained the wreckage and, as GT40 values rose, it was inevitably rebuilt. Owned and recently restored by Don Silawsky, of Washington DC, the car's gold colour scheme suits it admirably.

C12

C13

C14

C16

C13. Following Le Mans in 1966, this Mark II, formerly the Shelby team spare, was used in a series of Autolite advertisements..The car, which is probably XGT3, is campaigned with excellent results in vintage racing in the USA. Owned by Dale and Pat Nichols, of Orlando, Florida, it is one of very few Mark IIAs to survive in totally original condition.

C14. At Daytona in 1966 the works Mark IIs received coloured patches on the front bodywork, to help in their identification from the pits. At Sebring the same year the idea was taken further, with all the Mark IIs being painted different colours. A J Foyt and Ronnie Bucknum shared this Holman & Moody entry, which was fitted with a two-speed semi-automatic transmission. They finished twelfth, after delays caused by brake problems.

C15. Ford approached Daytona in 1967 with the confidence that befitted reigning champions. Shelby's Mark IIs were numbered 1, 2 and 3, and coloured yellow, blue and red respectively. The Holman & Moody entries were 4, 5 and 6, being gold, bronze and silver. This is the Andretti/Ginther car, which retired with the gearbox maladies which struck down the entire works entry. The only survivor was car number 1, of McLaren and Bianchi, which, its transmission replaced, limped to the finish in seventh place, behind GT40 road car 1049!

C15

C17

C18

C16. The X-1's sole race when rebodied as a Mark IIA roadster was at Sebring in 1966, where it achieved an unexpected victory following the last-minute retirement of another Mark II. Drivers were Ken Miles and Lloyd Ruby.

C17. 1080 saw service far from the beaten track, being used in both Portugal and Angola by its current owner, Emilio Marta, of Vilanova de Gaia, taking part in such events as the Benguela International 500 kilometres and the New Lisbon 6-hours. As late as 1973 the car was being used successfully in international events, Marta being classified third in the Angolan International Championship and first in the National Championship that year. Happily, both the car and its owner escaped the Angolan civil war, returning to Portugal in 1975. This illustration shows the car in its penultimate race, at Vila do Conde in 1979.

C18. Very few GT40s have been returned to the colour schemes they wore in their racing days, but the beautifully restored 1003 is one exception. This car was used extensively by Ford France during the mid 'sixties, and returned to France in 1976 for the annual Beaujolais "race". The car was in the lead between Paris and Calais whilst being driven by owner Robert J Horne, of London, when tyre problems forced its retirement.

C19. On GT40s the entire visible bodywork, with the exception of the roof, windscreen surrounds and roll-over structure, was unstressed fibreglass, and easily changeable; consequently their appearance could be, and often was, altered considerably. This car wears the Mark III style of front body, with quad-headlights in raised fenders, but is actually an early GT40, 1002. The tail section too is non-standard, apparently coming from Paul Hawkins' AMGT/2. Since this photo was taken in 1972, 1002 has been restored to standard configuration.

C19

C20. The first Graber finished road car, 1033, was sold by Filipinetti to Bolivian industrialist Ortiz Patino, and converted for racing use by his godson, Dominique Martin. The car is seen here in the paddock at Le Mans in 1969; it failed to make the start, due to engine trouble. It was retired from racing in early 1970 and was totally destroyed by fire later that year, the extent of the damage being such that it is highly unlikely ever to be rebuilt.

C20

C21. Unusual modifications are seen here on yet another Filipinetti car, the Scuderia's 1039. Its racing days over, it was converted by Franco Sbarro for road use, and featured a tan leather interior. The exhaust was lowered and a lift-up section incorporated in the tail, presumably to provide increased luggage space and better access. The car was photographed at Le Mans in 1968; note the tyres which look positively skinny by 1980s standards.

C21